NORTH YORK MOORS

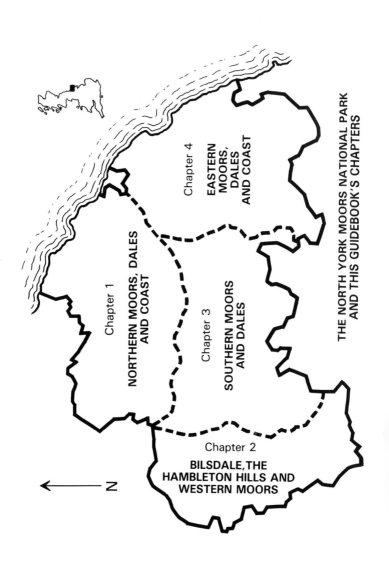

Chapter 1
NORTHERN MOORS, DALES AND COAST

Chapter 4
EASTERN MOORS, DALES AND COAST

Chapter 3
SOUTHERN MOORS AND DALES

Chapter 2
BILSDALE, THE HAMBLETON HILLS AND WESTERN MOORS

N ←

THE NORTH YORK MOORS NATIONAL PARK AND THIS GUIDEBOOK'S CHAPTERS

NORTH YORK MOORS

Walks In The National Park
by
Martin Collins

CICERONE PRESS
MILNTHORPE, CUMBRIA.

Acknowledgements

This book is dedicated to Diana, who shared the walking and contributed immeasurably to the process of transforming observations and ideas into guidebook form. Without her advice, encouragement, and above all her patience during the many months of preparation, the project may never have reached completion.

I would also like to thank individual contributors who kindly provided material on their long-distance and challenge walks; Sue Coles of the National Register of Long-distance Paths; Alan Stainforth at the National Park Information Service, Helmsley; Newcastle Weather Centre.

All photographs, maps and drawings by the author.

CONTENTS

Page

Chapter 3 - The Southern Moors and Dales 101

Chapter 4 - The Eastern Moors, Dales and Coast 139

Chapter 5 - Distance and Challenge Walks 197

PREFACE

One late summer morning while prospecting a walk for this book on the moors above Farndale, an impression which may have been forming for months finally took shape as a conscious thought. It was one of those unimpeachable days of sparkling light, the heather, now in full bloom, rolling into acid-purple, hard edged infinity. Climbing from the dale onto the moortops, I had passed no other fellow human and it was this above all else which triggered the realisation: here I stood, in as beautiful an upland landscape as any in Britain, never far from the population centres of York, Middlesborough, Tees-side and the coastal belt, yet I was totally alone.

The thought, simple though it was, echoed back in memory as a unifying thread running through many diverse experiences in this broad, open swath of North Yorkshire. For these moors have the capacity - an unenclosed generosity of space - to swallow all who visit them, so that even on the busiest summer weekends, freedom from noise and traffic is easily attainable.

More hospitable and strikingly lovelier than the Pennines 50 miles to the west, the North York Moors invite the walker, whatever his disposition and range, in ways which few other regions of Britain do. Gradients and terrain are friendly, but the plateau does not lack a challenge for those who seek it: within the miniature wilderness of the high tops, shunned by most roads, walking can be exposed and arduous, especially in winter.

Standing that morning amongst the heather, lulled by the lazy drone of honey bees, I realised, too, how relatively unwalked even the dales, forests and coast had been. It is as if there is simply too much magnificent country here for any one part to attract more than a sprinkling of people. Certainly there are paths and tracks in abundance throughout the National Park, but only those on well publicised routes seem to be regularly walked. Time after time in the most delectable spots, rights-of-way on the map were used scarcely enough to remain open and viable.

And so a conclusion emerged that whilst the ecological and visual scars of overuse are a problem on popular itineraries, there is scope almost without limit for exploration quite literally 'off the beaten track', in marvellously accessible and spirit-lifting surroundings. I have no desire to redress this happy imbalance (though a book such as this might tip the scales a little the other way). Indeed, I hope readers will be encouraged by experiences on these walks to look even further afield for new alternatives of their own in this most richly endowed area.

Martin Collins
January 1987

INTRODUCTION

About the North York Moors National Park

The North York Moors were designated a National Park in 1952, following the National Parks and Access to the Countryside Act of 1949. Over 80% of the land is in private ownership - farms, quarries, the National Trust, etc. - most of the remainder belonging to the Forestry Commission. Administration of the Park is controlled by a committee comprised of representatives from North Yorkshire and Cleveland County Councils, four District Councils and members appointed by the Secretary of State for the Environment. In common with other National Park Authorities, their principal duties are to protect the area's landscape and wildlife and to reconcile the public's increasing use of the park for recreational purposes with the interests of those such as farmers and foresters who live and work in it.

The Park's 553 square miles (1432 square kilometres) of heather moor, dales and sea-cliffs is roughly kidney-shaped, bounded by the Vale of Pickering to the south, the gently rolling Vales of York and Mowbray to the west, and the low-lying Tees estuary and North Sea coast to the north and east.

The moors rise dramatically from their surroundings to an average altitude of around 1200ft. (366m), almost 1500ft. (457m) at their highest point. It is one of the largest continuous moorland expanses in England, yet the National Park boundary also embraces a number of other diverse and distinctive regions: high sea cliffs, the long Cleveland Hills escarpment, undulating agricultural land, broad pastoral dales, steep wooded valleys and substantial tracts of conifer forest.

As reference to a map will immediately reveal, the North York Moors are, in fact, not one coherent massif of that name, but an amalgamation of local moors named after adjacent valleys or parishes. Despite the attentions of modern man, it is an ancient landscape, liberally scattered with relics from pre-history to the Industrial Revolution. Over 1100 miles (1770km) of public footpaths and bridleways criss-cross the area, in addition to green lanes, country roads and forestry tracks. Such ready access to richly interesting and varied terrain makes this one of Britain's finest walking locations.

On the high moors

There are few towns of any size within the National Park boundary; Thirsk, Guisborough, Whitby, Scarborough and Pickering are all situated just outside. Of small towns and villages, however, there are many, though apart from high farms at the valley heads, the moors themselves are uninhabited. The coastal strip from near Skinningrove to Cloughton is more evenly settled and attracts many thousands of visitors in its own right during the summer season.

The central moors, exposed and inhospitable in all but the kindest weather, are avoided by main roads, except for the A169 from Pickering to Whitby. Numerous 'B' roads lead through the dales and, in some places, over the tops, providing a good choice of starting points for walks. British Rail stations can be found at Scarborough, Thirsk and in villages along the Esk Valley line from Whitby to Middlesborough, while the privately-operated, mainly steam hauled North York Moors Railway runs from Pickering to Grosmont during the summer months and off-season weekends, calling at stations and halts in scenic Newton Dale.

Accomodation for visitors ranges from up-market hotels, through country inns, Bed-and-Breakfast establishments and youth hostels to caravan and campsites. On the whole, it is the latter categories rather than the former which the walker will encounter in the heart of the

Grosmont - northern terminus of the North York Moors Railway

National Park. The Ramblers' Association and Cyclists' Touring Club publish a yearly guide to Bed-and-Breakfasts, and the National Park Information Service will provide a list of accommodation on or near the Cleveland Way, including campsites. There are youth hostels at Helmsley, Osmotherley, Westerdale, Saltburn, Whitby, near Robin Hood's Bay, Wheeldale, Lockton and Scarborough.

Farms will often take overnight lightweight campers for a nominal charge, and details of formal campsites in the region are obtainable by joining the Camping and Caravanning Club of Great Britain. Remembering that nearly all land in the National Park is privately owned, every attempt should be made to seek permission before pitching a tent. For the addresses of organisations mentioned above, please turn to 'Useful Addresses'.

Walking Conditions, Clothing and Equipment

From the moor tops in a mid-winter storm to sheltered woodland on a balmy summer's afternoon, an enormous potential range of walking conditions may be encountered in the North York Moors National Park. Even on the same day, while one walker is exploring dale or forest in relative comfort, his counterpart on the tops could well be engaged in a struggle against the elements in which proper equipment and survival skills are of the essence. As in all upland regions of Britain, the advice is: 'Go prepared'.

Paths and tracks on the moortops are frequently stony, but where there is an overlay of peat they can be boggy and easily eroded. Off

11

The old coach road on Rudland Rigg

these paths, deep heather makes progress tiring and ankle or knee injuries more likely from unseen holes. Rough, motorable tracks, built mainly for grouse-shooting parties and not universally welcomed by the walking fraternity, nevertheless often link up with old coach roads and ancient trackways to form distinct walking routes over the high tops.

In summer, rampant bracken obscures some stretches of path, especially on the moorside approaches. Under snow cover too, paths can vanish altogether, heightening the need for navigation skills.

The moortops themselves form vast sweeps of gently undulating country, but descent into the dales or down the escarpment is often made through craggy outcrops or landslips. Rarely, however, are gradients as steep as in true mountain terrain and there is far less risk of getting into difficulties. On the North York Moors, exposure to weather and exhaustion are more likely hazards.

In the valley bottoms and on lower slopes in the south and east of the region, the only real inconvenience can be wet-weather mud on agricultural land and in woods. Rights of way through farms should be followed carefully, especially in the vicinity of stock or sown crops.

A summer's day above Farndale

Not all map-marked paths are well walked.

On the coast, paths can be slippery and there are several quite steep sections. Special care is needed where cliffs are falling away from the effects of erosion and on all cliff-edge paths in windy weather. Walkers are strongly advised to be aware of tide cycles so as not to be stranded while walking along beaches.

Although it can be as warm and sunny as anywhere in Britain, characteristic weather over the North York Moors tends to favour pursuits such as walking more than those relying on warm or settled conditions.

During spring and early summer, especially in the daytime, there is a high frequency of winds blowing off a chilly North Sea, with a predictable effect on air temperatures! The warmest months are June to September, with June topping the average daily sunshine league at 6.1 hours, closely followed by May (5.7 hours) and July (5.2 hours). June is also the driest summer month, though March is drier over the year as a whole. It is worth bearing in mind that temperatures given in general forecasts should be reduced by at least 2°C, since much of the Park lies at over 1000ft (304m) above sea level.

August, November and January are the wettest months on average (the August mean of 3.6″ (91mm) no more welcomed by walkers than anyone else!). Over 40″ (1000mm) can be expected as a typical year's total precipitation.

At 500-600ft (150-180m) above sea level, snow lies for an average of 30 days in a year, but there can be wide variations from one year to the next. On the high moors, the figure is often well in excess of 45 days. The last frost encountered is usually in mid-May, with a growing season from early April to late November, and grazing from mid April to mid September.

Mean wind speed for the region is 8.5mph, with gales (Force 8 or above) on some 10 days a year. Wind direction is partly determined by local topography, and tree shelter belts give good clues as to the commonest blows experienced. Many are aligned to give protection from northerlies, while some funnelling of easterlies occurs between the moors and the Wolds/Howardian Hills to the south, and to a lesser extent along the Esk Valley in the north.

The coast is exposed to winds from north-west to east-south-east with a long fetch over open water: not only does this depress temperatures there during spring and early summer when the North Sea is still very cold, but wind speeds of Force 6 and above are more common than further inland.

Experienced walkers will have their own tried-and-tested outdoor gear and will readily assess a walk's requirements: those newer to walking may not feel so confident. The following notes are simply intended to remind anyone embarking on a walk of some duration in the National Park to make adequate preparations, particularly if it involves going onto the tops.

Well-fitting, comfortable boots add immeasurably to the pleasure of walking, as well as providing support and protection in all conditions. Two pairs of socks will minimise blisters, while anklets or full length gaiters are useful in rain or snow. Other clothing will depend on the season and prevailing weather, though in general terms, several thin layers are more versatile than one thick one and at least a spare sweater should be carried in summer. Shell clothing - cagoule and overtrousers - are almost indispensable for protection from wind and wet, a lethal combination which can lead to the onset of hyperthermia if not guarded against - even in summer.

Though not a characteristic of the north-east of England, when it does occur, continuous hot sunshine can pose the threat of heat stroke and dehydration on protracted hikes. (At such times, special care is also needed to avoid starting a moorland fire.) Loose, light clothing and a brimmed hat are the order of the day, not forgetting a good sized water-bottle.

Winter expeditions on the tops should always be treated seriously.

Clothing and equipment needs to be able to withstand potentially severe weather conditions, as do the walkers wearing them. Extra necessities include woolly hat (an uncovered head acts like a big radiator, discharging up to a quarter of the body's heat), gloves, energy rations, torch and whistle, survival bag or tent, hot drinks in a flask, more spare clothing.

Two other indispensable items, winter or summer, are a first-aid kit and map and compass. The former will spend nearly all its time in the rucsac, but the latter will need carrying in a map case for periodic reference, as will this book!

Always try to obtain an up-to-date weather bulletin before setting out. Overall trends can be ascertained from television and radio forecasts, though temperature and wind speed values generally pertain to Britain's densely populated urban and lowland regions where the majority of viewers/listeners live. For more accurate predictions about local weather on the North York Moors, a recorded telephone service is available by ringing (091) 246 8091.

Finally, in the unhappy event of accident, serious injury and illness, or the verified loss of a fellow walker, write down the map reference of your position and call the Police by dialling 999 from the nearest phone. The Police will advise the best course of action and may call out a Search and Rescue Team.

Should you be the unfortunate one being rescued, find a sheltered spot, put on all spare clothing, use a survival bag if carried, eat some emergency food and make the International Distress Call - 6 long torch flashes or whistle blasts repeated at one minute intervals. The answer is 3 flashes or blasts at one minute intervals. If you are benighted, it may be necessary to wait for daylight before help arrives or can be sent for. Although walking alone has its advantages, going in small groups greatly increases safety on more ambitious outings. It is always advisable to inform someone at home or base about an intended itinerary and to let them know a safe return has been made.

About this Guide
Only a guidebook several times the size of this one could exhaustively cover all walking possibilities within the North York Moors National Park. Even then, individual corners of the countryside - favourite itineraries of some walkers perhaps - might fail to get included: the permutations are just too numerous!

In compiling this book of 45 specially selected and recently verified walks, the author has kept two goals in mind: to provide a more or less even spread of routes throughout the Park area, and to connect each

The Vale of Mowbray from the Cleveland Hills escarpment

walk to one or more features of interest, be it outstanding scenery, prehistoric site, relics of old industry, historic building or ancient trackway.

Indeed, there is so much to see that the enterprising walker armed with the appropriate map could well devise extensions to the walks to take in additional places. Since the majority of routes are circular, starting points can be varied too.

Some rights of way marked on the map have fallen into disuse and vanished beneath heather or thickets, which seriously impede progress and can make nonsense of a planned itinerary. By unravelling those that have disappeared from those that haven't, at least on the walks covered by this guide, the author hopes to save readers many frustrating and fruitless forays casting about for non-existent paths. Indeed, where necessary, route directions are quite detailed, freeing readers from unnecessary equivocation and thereby, it is hoped, increasing their appreciation of the environment and the activity of walking itself.

The majority of walks in this book can be completed easily in a day, some in just 2 or 3 hours: the longer ones might not fit so comfortably into winter daylight hours, however. Distances are given, along with approximate timings based on an unhurried pace with occasional pauses, but not, of course, including longer stops for meals, etc.

An attempt has been made to grade the walks, not that this can ever be achieved with total objectivity. Even so, some indication of how demanding a route is likely to be is helpful when planning where to go and who to take along. 'Easy' denotes suitable for whole family (with discretion) and no need for specialised outdoor gear beyond common-sense footwear and warm clothing. (Better source for this category of walk would be National Park leaflets describing specially devised short family rambles and obtainable from the National Park Information Service. See 'Useful Addresses').

'Moderate' grading implies a mixture of walking terrain, from lanes and farm tracks to rough paths over heather moor, involving the kind of ascent, descent and exposure to weather which one would expect in an upland region. 'More strenuous' simply means an increase in gradients, awkward terrain, length, or combination of all three factors. (For really hard routes, refer to the chapter on Long Distance and Challenge Walks!)

Finally, mention is made at its beginning if stretches of a walk are at high level and therefore exposed to the effects of inclement weather: wind, rain, mist, snow, etc. Maps are all drawn to scale and can be confidently used to assess progress and position, preferably in conjunction with a suitable OS sheet. Recommended maps are:- 1″ OS Tourist Map of the North York Moors (best for planning); 1:25,000 Outdoor Leisure Maps, North York Moors - NW/SW Sheet and NE/SE Sheet.

The author has divided the National Park into 4 regions. A brief summary of each appears at the beginning of their respective chapters, along with a map locating the walks, which have all been given a number for easy reference.

To save the reader from wading through chunks of text dealing with background information (views, points of interest, etc.) while trying to follow route directions, all such material is printed in italics. Route directions appear in normal type.

For the sake of brevity, abbreviations have been used thus:-
R = right; L = left; N = north; S = south; E = east; W = west.

KEY TO MAPS

 HAMLET, VILLAGE OR TOWN

PUBLIC ROAD

FARM LANE, PRIVATE DRIVE OR
GOOD MOOR TRACK

 FOOTPATH OR LESS DISTINCT TRACK

 LAKE, COAST, GILL,
BECK
OR RIVER

 HILLTOP, CRAG, MOORLAND CROSS

NOTABLE RELIGIOUS RUIN, BUILDINGS

 DISUSED RAILWAY, OPERATING
RAILWAY

CHAPTER 1

THE NORTHERN MOORS,
DALES AND COAST

This chapter extends to the National Park's northern boundary, from Ingleby Greenhow and Great Ayton in the west, north past Guisborough, and east to the coast near Loftus. Its southern limit follows the main North York Moors watershed, but veers back to the Esk valley at Egton Bridge, picking up the National Park boundary again (which excludes Whitby) to the coast at Sandsend.

The area's rolling moorland masses, highest to the south near the watershed, are split west to east by Esk Dale, and south by the tributary valleys of Danby Dale, Little and Great Fryup Dales and Glaisdale. The intervening ridges ('riggs'), leading to the loftiest moorland, provide an exhilarating foil to the gentler, more agricultural landscapes in the dale bottoms.

Except in the west, there is relatively little forestry. The moors are clothed extensively with heather and ling, while field patterns, meadow and dry-stone walling characterise the dales. Footpaths, bridleways and country lanes abound, many with origins as ancient as the enigmatic stones, crosses and tumuli which they pass.

Although on a map quite close to Tees-side, the Heritage Coast in this section is largely unspoilt and full of interest, taking in several old fishing villages, spectacular cliff scenery and relics of long-dead industrial activity. The track bed of the disused Yorkshire Coast Railway adds variety to the walking routes.

Excursions in this northern part of the National Park are perhaps the most varied of all. They range from easy valley strolls suitable for the whole family to challenging moorland circuits for the more committed walker. Danby Lodge Moors Centre, plum in the middle of this area, will act as a magnet for most visitors - a pleasant and rewarding day can be spent there, viewing exhibitions and enjoying the amenities.

British Rail's Esk Valley service provides a rail link between villages in the dale, as well as connecting with other destinations. Many ramblers use it to return to base at the end of a day, or to reach a starting point without the need to park a vehicle - not always a simple matter on the narrow, twisting lanes. A few roads run up over the moors, giving access to the tops without a preceding ascent. The only fast roads in the area are the A171 Guisborough to Whitby, and the A174 coast road: elsewhere, progress can be unexpectedly slow on the tortuous 'B' roads.

The Walks

Walk 1 explores the moors above Guisborough, culminating in an ascent of Roseberry Topping and a vist to Captain Cook's Monument on Easby Moor. Walk 2, a longer and more demanding circuit, climbs from Kildale onto Battersby Moor and makes a big loop round remote Baysdale Moor before flanking Baysdale itself and climbing back over Kildale Moor. Walk 3 from Castleton and Westerdale leads to two famous stone crosses on the moortop and returns via Botton, an impressive Camphill Trust village, and Danby Dale.

The source of the River Esk, high on Westerdale Moor, is reached on Walk 4, followed by a visit to the Lion Inn on Blakey Rigg and a walk along the track bed of the old Rosedale Ironstone Railway. Danby Lodge Moors Centre forms the start for Walks 5 and 6. Walk 5 climbs over Danby Rigg, up round the head of Great Fryup Dale and over into Little Fryup Dale, returning along by the River Esk. Walk 6 contours above Esk Dale to Lealholm (possible return by train) and back over Beacon Hill. There are numerous short, waymarked walks in and around Esk Dale starting from the Moors Centre, where the very good explanatory leaflets may be obtained.

Glaisdale Rigg is mounted on the ancient Whitby Road and Glaisdale itself circled by Walk 7. Walk 8 combines lovely woods just inland with a visit to the fascinating fishing village of Staithes - one of the real gems of Yorkshire's Heritage Coast - completing the circuit along magnificent cliffs. Finally, from picturesque Runswick, a beach walk leads up to the cliff tops and the site of a Roman Signal Station, the return leg of Walk 9 being along the dismantled Yorkshire Coast Railway.

WALK 1   LONSDALE PLANTATION - SLEDDALE - HIGHCLIFF NAB - ROSEBERRY TOPPING - CAPTAIN COOK'S MONUMENT - LONSDALE PLANTATION

9½ miles (15.5km) - 4½ hours - Moderate but more strenuous in places.

This walk starts from the end of the metalled B road (gated) which leaves the Kildale-Commondale road 1½ miles (2.4km) E of Kildale at Percy Rigg. *There is limited parking space at the road end or on verges.*

Walk SE back along this ribbon of tarmac on Kildale Moor, alongside Lonsdale Plantation, for about ½ mile (800m) and turn L on the 'Private Road to Sleddale' (referring to motorists). The partly surfaced track runs over heather moor and drops round over Sleddale Slack. At the final bend to Sleddale Farm, turn L up a good track which gradually climbs the E slopes of Codhill Heights towards a conspicuous gap in the edge of the forest ahead.

The way trends L onto a broad stretch of open moorland. Fork L on a grassier track, aiming towards a clump of tall deciduous trees at the L end of forest. Here, go through a handgate in the wall corner and fork R in woods, crossing a ride to the craggy outcrop of Highcliff Nab (981ft, 300m).*From here there are good views N over Guisborough and beyond to the Tees.*

Retrace steps to the handgate at the edge of moor and turn R down by a wall, now on the route of the Cleveland Way (though in the opposite direction to normal). The path becomes marshy down beyond Highcliff Farm. At a sheep dip in a wall corner, bear L by a direction post, cross a plank bridge and climb up through bracken onto Hutton Moor. The route swings R and meets a broad track. *(If needs be, the walk can be short-cut here by turning L and reaching the starting point in about ¾ miles (1.25km).*

Turn R and at the edge of the forest pass through a gate and turn L inside the fence (though a well trodden path also runs outside it). Continue along the forest edge to a corner, where bear L through a gate by a post and proceed ahead over Newton Moor. *Cresting a rise, a dramatic view unfolds - from the steep hump of Roseberry Topping directly ahead, round to Captain Cook's Monument to the south and beyond it the great sweep of the Cleveland Hills' northern escarpment.*

22

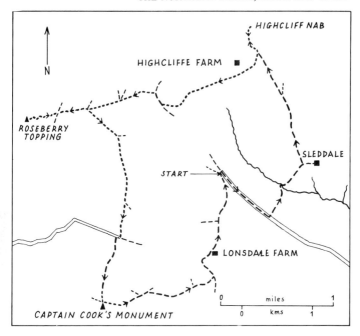

Go through a wall gate and walk down the rutted, much used track which can be seen climbing unmistakably to Roseberry Topping's rocky little summit. *Once the site of an ancient beacon, the hill's distinctive shape has been sharpened by quarrying for jet, iron-ore and stone, with the associated overgrown workings still visible. It is hoped that an Appeal, launched by the National Trust, who have recently acquired the site, and supported by the naturalist David Bellamy, will finance much-needed work on paths, fences, woodland and bracken control around this popular landmark.*

½ mile (800m) to the south stands Airy Holme Farm, where Captain Cook spent part of his boyhood. Paths radiate up Roseberry Topping from all directions, the other main access points being from car parks near Newton-under-Roseberry on the A173 to the west.

Return to the gate on Newton Moor and turn R along the wall above Slacks Wood. Our next destination is Captain Cook's Monument, clearly visible to the S. Following the wall along Great Ayton Moor for 1¼ miles (2km), it drops to a car parking/picnic area at the end of a

23

Roseberry Topping

lane from Great Ayton. Go through a gate ahead R and climb the very wide, rather eroded track through trees, ending in steps onto Eastby Moor top.

The tall stone obelisk commemorating Captain Cook's achievements was erected in 1827. Born in 1728, the great circumnavigator was originally apprenticed to a draper in Staithes at the age of 12, before starting his life at sea on colliers. His enthusiasm for navigation gained him entry to the Royal Navy at age 27, and he subsequently joined several expeditions to what were then the new lands of Canada and Newfoundland. So great was his reputation as a navigator by the mid-1700's that he commanded surveys of the Australian coast and went on to explore and chart the Pacific South Sea Islands. He was killed at Hawaii on February 14th, 1779.

There is a small museum in Great Ayton's schoolroom where he learned navigational mathematics, and more material in Pannett Park Library, Whitby. For those wishing to trace Captain Cook's association with this part of Yorkshire in more detail, a Cook Heritage Trail was set up in 1978 - the 250th anniversary of his birth. It connects such places of interest as his birthplace at Marton, Middlesborough, his father's grave at Marske, his early shopkeeping days in Staithes, and Whitby, where he began his career as a seaman.

Captain Cook's Monument

Turning E from the monument, our route approaches a plantation corner, goes through a wall and a fence and contours ahead in larch forest. Ignoring tracks L and R, stay on the surfaced forest road to a gate, where the Cleveland Way route turns abruptly R down towards Kildale. We turn L here, through mature conifers and down, veering R out past Londsdale Farm.

Once over Lonsdale Beck, the farm road swings L at a group of barns. Keep straight on through a gate and up a stony track. Ignore a R turn ('No Vehicles') and climb alongside, then through, Lonsdale Plantation (signed 'Lownsdale' at the top), to emerge at the starting point.

WALK 2 KILDALE - BAYSDALE ABBEY
- ARMOUTH WATH - HOGRAH MOORS
-BAYSDALE - LEVEN VALE - KILDALE

---

14 miles (23km) - 6 to 7 hours - More strenuous; exposed to bad weather in parts; map and compass skills advised.

From Kildale village, walk W on the Easby road for 500m and turn L up a metalled lane, signed cul-de-sac. *This lane takes little traffic and climbs high onto Battersby Moor, leaving the walker free to admire unfolding views of outstanding quality as height is gained.* The lane passes through 2 gates and ascends steadily for some 1½ miles (2.5km): it is part of the Cleveland Way route.

On the moor top, about 250m beyond the second gate, look out for a stout wooden post on the R and a faint trod through heather off L opposite. This soon becomes more distinct and passes through a wall gap by a tree. Follow the wall down L to a bend in the road servicing Baysdale Farm, go past the farm buildings and continue on the surfaced track towards the large grey profile of Baysdale Abbey. *The farm here stands on the site of a 12th century Cistercian nunnery, but all that remain are a medieval ribbed bridge and a few sculptured stones. (A short-cut is possible from behind the farm - climb across 2 fields E to Thorntree House, missing out Armouth Wath).*

From a field corner gate just in front of the large grey building, walk SW up over pasture to a gap between fence and wall. The way now climbs Middle Head, slanting ½-R up to a gate and a broken stile. Go through and fork R on the plainer track, up through bracken and a sparsely planted plantation, through another gate and out onto open moor. Keep R at a fork and enjoy the good, springy turf as the path ascends the E flank of Middle Head ridge above the wooded valley of Grain Beck.

At a junction *(the path R doubles back NW over Ingleby Moor and down the escarpment at Ingleby Bank)*, keep straight on, descending over increasingly wet and reedy ground on the line of the old Flagged Road. *Armouth Wath is a derelict sheepfold in an impressively remote situation where streams draining the surrounding moors converge into Grain Beck and thence into Baysdale. Oddly enough, this sense of isolation is illusory, since both the clear Cleveland Way route along Greenhow Bank, and Ingleby Incline leading to populated farmland below the escarpment, are less than a mile away (1.5km) to the SW.*

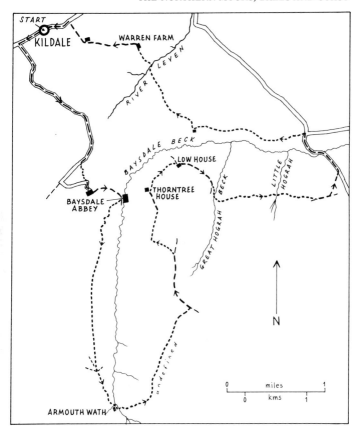

Tiny stone bridges span 2 becks at the end of a belt of trees and beyond them, the route climbs E, steeply at first, then out onto Stockdale Moor, swinging gradually more N (any trod followed should be confirmed by a compass bearing). In a mile or so, a plainer path is joined at a heap of stones, in a direction just E of N and keeping to the R of higher ground (Nicholas Ruck). We soon meet a broad, stony track used by shooting parties, along which turn L. *Wide views extend in all directions, with Roseberry Topping and Captain Cook's Monument visible on the northern skyline.*

27

Bridge over Great Hograh Beck

In just over ½ mile (800m) of gradual descent, take a thin path forking L in a shallow groove to the corner of a wire fence. *(An alternative short-cut is to continue on the track for another 100m or so and fork off R on a magnetic bearing of 225 deg. across rough heather moor to the E of Holiday Hill, joining the main route at Great Hograh Beck. However, walkers are advised that this is not a right of way.)*

Follow the fence down to the plantation edge, turn R, and at a gate go ½-L down a good forest track to Thorntree House. Before the building, turn R across grass to a gate in a wall corner. Beyond it, the route skirts just below a wall along 2 fields, with rampant bracken above and many young grouse around in summer. Cross a wall stile, go through a gate and follow the forest edge down and up to The Low House (or Shepherds House on some maps). Go over the stile, cross the lawn and pass through a gate, continuing forward up a forest track which leaves the tree edge for open heather moor, swinging round progressively R (S).

A thin path forks L towards the top end of trees at Great Hograh Beck and leads to a delightful miniature stone bridge, dated 1938 and paved with slabs. *In fine weather, one could hardly find a more pleasant picnic spot than here by the beck.* On the other side, continue in the same direction for about 50m, then bear ½-L on a thin but distinct path E over heather and bracken. *This is the ancient Skinner Howe Cross Road, though at a boot's width, hardly a road! To left and right, various large rocks and standing stones punctuate the slopes of Great Hograh Moor.*

After several hundred metres, Little Hograh Beck is crossed and after the same distance again, the path reaches the narrow John Breckon Road at a small cairn. Turn L and in 500m join the Westerdale-Kildale road, down which turn L to cross Baysdale Beck at a ford and footbridge, with plentiful parking space and grassy levels for a picnic.

300m up the other side, take a good track off the road L, through bracken and contouring along the S flank of Kildale Moor. *The beauty and wildness of Baysdale can be well appreciated: with no road in the valley itself, the few inhabitants reach Kildale along the narrow moor road over Battersby Moor which formed the first leg of this walk.* At a derelict farm building, leave the boundary wall and take a line up R off the corner, threading up over heather and bracken in a generally NW direction. Once over the top and through a gate, the path heads downhill past drainage channels to a small conifer plantation in Leven Vale.

The upper waters of Eskdale, in particular Lonsdale Beck and the short River Leven which rises just to the south-west, flow unexpectedly west, rather than east along the Esk valley which completely dissects the National Park from Kildale to Whitby.

Cross the Leven and climb to Warren Farm, leaving the buildings L(W) on the farm lane through Little Kildale Wood. Just beyond Little Kildale, turn R down Green Gate Lane and L along the road back to Kildale village.

WALK 3 CASTLETON - WESTERDALE - YOUNG RALPH CROSS & FAT BETTY - DANBY HIGH MOOR - BOTTON - DANBY DALE - CASTLETON

12½ miles (20km) - 5 to 6 hours - More strenuous; partly exposed in bad weather. Map and compass skills advised.

Castleton is one in a string of delightful villages served by British Rail's Esk Valley line. From the centre, walk uphill SW along the road, past Moorlands Hotel. Where the main road swings L immediately beyond a R fork to Commondale, keep straight on along a narrow, unfenced road towards Westerdale. *There are good views of this dale and the moors to the west.*

At the fork by a post-box, take a thin grassy trod down R through bracken past a disused quarry L. This descends to the R of a wall, then drops R to the road. Cross over and continue on down on a good grassy track, ignoring a path off L. At a gate, turn sharp L and descend through bracken to a footbridge over Whyett Beck, after which a thin path is followed up ½-L, climbing pleasantly above a small wood. Out onto stony, bilberry and brackeny moorland, the clear track proceeds ahead, wall on L. Shortly after passing a Scots Pine plantation on the L, cross a big wall stile and aim slightly L ahead to a wall gap, passing below more pines.

Still on the flanks of Westerdale Moor, the route now passes through a metal gate and continues with wall on L towards Dale View Farm. 2 gates later, go up R into the outer farmyard, through it and onto a farm road to the public road just N of Westerdale village. Turn L downhill, past a sports field, over the River Esk adjacent to Hunters' Stee, a medieval packhorse bridge, and steeply up to the village centre. *Westerdale Youth Hostel was once a romantic Victorian shooting lodge down by the river.*

Turn L along a lane at the top of the village and almost instantly turn R, diagonally across 2 fields through stone stiles, meeting a farm road (Broad Gate Road), along which turn R up to Broad Gate Farm. Maintaining a SE direction, follow the track down by fields to a small footbridge over Tower Beck. Here, turn R then L, up fields by the boundary wall to Dale Head Farm, with the steep edge of Castleton Rigg now ahead. Keep R of the buildings and continue on up the clear bridleway to the moor top and the public road at High Crag. *It's worth*

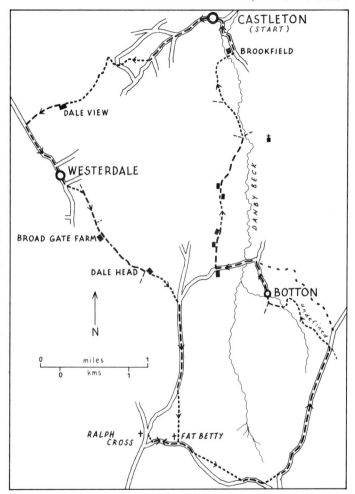

crossing over, for the views down Danby Dale are marvellous.

Walk S along the road for just over ½ mile. (1.1km) and watch for a post L where the road bends R. From here a narrow path rises gently over open moor, due S, past the odd boundary stone and over to meet

31

Danby Dale from High Crag

the Rosedale road at Fat Betty. *This ancient wayside cross signifies the conjunction of Danby, Rosedale and Westerdale parish boundaries and is one of the best known crosses on the North York Moors. Officially called White Cross on O.S. maps, the distinctive name of Fat Betty differentiates it from another White Cross above Commondale. Fat Betty is an appropriately descriptive title for this squat white socket stone bearing a wheelhead cross which, on repeated visits, is soon regarded as an old friend.*

Turn R along the road for a short detour to Ralph Cross. In 400m, just beyond a viewpoint pull-in, short-cut the road junction by taking a trod off R (NW). In 200m this leads out to Young Ralph Cross, chosen as the emblem of the National Park and incorporated into its official logo. *Old Ralph Cross, a much smaller affair, lies a few hundred metres to the SW amongst the heather.*

These ancient crosses, of medieval origin, are surrounded by mystery and enigma and may well have replaced standing stones of even greater antiquity. They appear in locations all over the North York Moors and probably mark old boundaries and routes across the tops. Before roads, such navigational markers would have been useful and occasionally lifesaving.

Fat Betty

Retrace steps to Fat Betty and continue along the road to the next bend. Before a water-filled hollow, a good track forks off L (SE), short-cutting the road; when it is rejoined, walk along it for about 250m and take another short-cut L to reach the Danby road. (If in doubt, simply turn L at the next road junction.)

Our route now follows the Danby road, a narrow, quiet ribbon of tarmac E of N, over Seavey Hill and gently downhill. In a little over 1¼ miles (2.2km), look out carefully for a small boulder on the L, opposite an overgrown rutted track coming in from the R (S). Turn L here (map ref: NZ 705034) on a very thin path over heather, soon confirmed by a sunken groove, the original bridleway, and a heap of

33

Ralph Cross, near Rosedale Head

stones. *(If this turn should be missed, watch for a small pile of stones 250m further on. A thin path NW over heather leaves here and heads towards crags just visible ahead L. The path drops into a hollow way downhill through bracken towards a copse. At a signpost by the intake wall, go through the gate L and down to Botton Farm. Go straight down the lane and turn L into Botton village.)*

On the main route, a compass bearing of 330 deg. magnetic over an area of cleared heather will lead to a continuation of the sunken groove, which drops more steeply to the R of Old Hannah's Nick stream valley towards Botton, now clearly seen below. Pass through a waymarked gate, over pasture above an old wall to a wooden footbridge. Cross a fence and go along a plantation edge to a stile L into a field. Follow the tree edge and at a wall, go over a stile R. Now walk down L of a small stream and through a gate in the bottom L hand corner. Cross ½-R to another gate and go L round a wall on a track which veers R down to Falcon Farm. Go through the farmyard and R onto a metalled lane. Where this turns L, go R by a white fence over Old Hannah's Nick and out at Botton Hall, turning R into the village.

As visitors soon discover, Botton is no ordinary village. As part of the Association of Camphill Communities for the Mentally Handicapped, it offers a unique environment in which 'patients' and 'staff' play equal parts in the life and work of the community. Many villagers work in small production units making such things as dolls, cheeses, bread, wooden toys, printed material, glassware and textiles. There are also 4 farms, plus gardens and a forestry section. For the 150 or so mentally handicapped people at Botton, work is both therapeutic in establishing new skills and responsibilities, as well as commercially important to the village's continued success: standards are high and the community is not far short of self-sufficiency. However, donations, subscriptions and covenants from the general public are vital to the project's long-term survival.

In the village centre are coffee bar and shops selling books, gifts, glassware and other products made here; there is also a new creamery and food centre, and a Post Office.

Leave Botton on the village lane N towards Danby and at the road junction, turn L across Danby Beck and uphill past a phone box and small Wesleyan Chapel (circa 1855). At Stormy Hall Farm, take the public bridleway R by a millstone. The good stony track passes through Blackmires Farm and on to West Cliff Farm. From here, follow a grassy track through a gate and along a field edge with a wall on the L. Cross a stone stile, wall now on R, past a rowan tree and over another stone stile into a grassy walled lane.

Proceed ahead past Plum Tree Farm yard and along the surfaced lane to West Green Farm. Continue down the lane and at a T-junction keep L. *(A short detour R can be made to look at Danby Church, up to the L of a small wood.)* Pass through gates above Danby Beck and keep straight on, over a boggy stretch, gates leading gradually away from the stream uphill - a very agricultural stretch of the walk!

Castleton is now visible on the ridge ahead as the way follows a muddy brook to the L, the path obscure. After crossing a large field, come down to a gate and, 100m beyond, a signpost. Go forward on a bridleway, over a brook and through a gate, heading up towards Brookfield Farm and into the yard. At the public road (Wandels Lane), turn L and walk into Castleton.

35

WALK 4   UPPER WESTERDALE - ESKLETS - MARGERY BRADLEY STONE - LION INN, BLAKEY - COURSE OF THE ROSEDALE IRON-STONE RAILWAY - HOWDALE HILL - UPPER WESTERDALE

8½ miles (13.5km) - 4 to 5 hours - More strenuous: sound footwear and map and compass skills advised. Exposed in bad weather.

Parking is limited in Upper Westerdale: the walk starts at the narrow road end near Wood End and care should be taken not to obstruct access to farms and fields, or to inconvenience passing traffic, including tractors.

From the road end, turn L towards Waites House Farm then immediately R on a surfaced lane to where footbridge and ford cross the infant Esk. Do not cross here, instead turning L onto a muddy path along the river's E bank, signed 'Footpath to Farndale'. Follow this, passing a stile then a gate and climbing along above the Esk through bracken, before gradually approaching it again and crossing on a good footbridge.

Now on the W bank (still boggy in places where feeder streams are negotiated), the path climbs away and well back from the Esk at the head of this truly delightful and remote valley. Our route passes 2 fields enclosed by ruined walls, and the completely derelict buildings of Esklets. Continue on the track to where it crosses a tributary stream: here we forsake the plain track climbing R, branching off L instead, across a field to trees and keeping L of a reedy area.

Our clearly visible path now crosses the headwaters of the Esk (for the last time!), goes through a wall gap, on through another, and at a white-tipped post turns L up a field edge with a wall on the L. At the next white-tipped post (old Lyke Wake Walk markers), veer slightly R, heading for 2 gaps in walls ahead. White arrows on rocks also mark the path in places.

Beyond the wall gaps, the old moorland path deteriorates somewhat but is never in doubt, climbing more determinedly and providing the best kind of rough walking. Cross what remains of High Hill Top intake wall and continue forward (E). The path improves, finally emerging at the Margery Bradley stone beside the Castleton road above Rosedale Head.

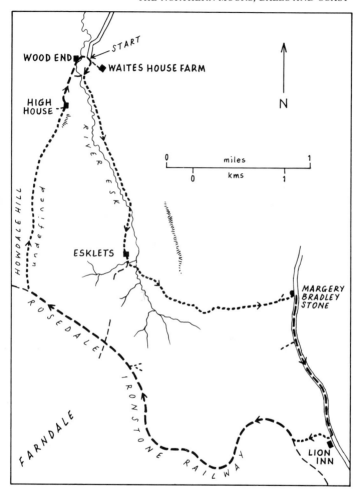

Turning R, a mile's striding out brings us to the Lion Inn. *A glimpse at the 1:25,000 map reveals a veritable peppering of old workings in the vicinity and, indeed, the Lion Inn was once patronised by coal and iron-stone miners. Behind the inn can be found Cockpit Howe, a bronze-age burial mound. The central hollow made by early grave robbers was used for*

37

Near the headwaters of the River Esk

cock fighting from the 17th to the 19th centuries. Nowadays the pub is a popular refreshment stop for walkers and motorists alike on these bleak moortops: at 1325ft (403m) above sea level, it is one of the highest in England.

Just before the inn buildings, our route turns R and cuts down (W) to join the track bed of the Rosedale Ironstone Railway. *(For more information, please turn to Walks 24 & 26 and Appendix 3.) Many walkers use its easy course - it forms part of several long-distance hikes, including the Coast to Coast and the Lyke Wake Walk - and while on it, no navigation is needed, even in the thickest 'roak' (the local name of Scandinavian origin for a heavy mist blowing in from the North Sea): in such conditions, knowing where to leave the track bed would be quite another matter!*

The track bed loops round the head of Farndale, past a sign R for the Esk Valley Way *(a short-cut down to Esklets and back to the start)*. In just under 3 miles (4.8km) from the Lion Inn, beyond a very shallow cutting before the track curves L *(Farndale is back in view to the S)*, turn off R on a thin path. (map ref: 645014).

This path, a little E of N, gives out at some shooting butts and the way ahead is over almost flat, trackless heather and bilberry. However, keep to the R (E) of Howdale Hill, ascending only a modest amount before Waites House Farm appears in view across Upper Westerdale. Begin dropping slightly R towards it, cross some boggy patches, and keep just above rowan trees to the R of The Nab. (NOTE: It is dangerous, especially in poor visibility, to descend too soon here, as there is a line of low crags below, not shown on maps.)

About 100m beyond the rowans, a good track is met descending off the moor and crossing 2 fields to High House Farm. Go through the gate below the farmyard (the many barking dogs are usually chained up!) and on down the metalled farm drive. Cross White Gill at a ford and turn R to the road at Wood End.

Red Grouse

WALK 5   DANBY LODGE MOORS CENTRE - AINTHORPE - DANBY RIGG - TROUGH HOUSE - GREAT FRYUP DALE - CRAG WOOD - MOORS CENTRE

13½ miles (22km) - 5½ to 6 hours - More strenuous; exposed in parts in bad weather.

Housed in a handsome former shooting lodge just to the east of Danby, the Moors Centre offers visitors an impressive array of facilities and information, all free of charge. Open daily between Easter and October, and on winter weekends, the building contains a large exhibition area, a book and souvenir shop and a cafeteria. A daily programme of illustrated talks with slides and films is augmented by guided walks, Nature and Family Activity trails and Brass Rubbing. Group visits are welcome provided they are booked in advance. (Danby Lodge National Park Centre, Lodge Lane, Danby, Whitby YO21 2NB; tel. Castleton (02876) 654.)

The lodge is surrounded by 13 acres of meadow, woodland, formal gardens and picnic area bordering the River Esk, and there is an adventure playground for children. Car parking is generous and free, and provision is made for the disabled.

A good day out can be enjoyed here without moving a muscle; however, Danby is an excellent centre from which to explore Upper Eskdale and there is much of interest for the walker throughout the adjacent moors and dales.

Danby itself was the home of Canon Atkinson, the local vicar for 53 years and author of the classic '40 Years in a Moorland Parish'. To the south-east stand the remains of Danby Castle, while down the dale away from the village, Danby church contains features from several centuries.

From the main entrance opposite the Moors Centre car park, a signed path leaves SW alongside the picnic area fence, crosses the River Esk and the railway line and leads to a minor road (Easton Lane). Turn R and walk along to Ainthorpe. Turn R to cross a tributary stream, then L towards Castleton, forking L almost immediately. Walk up past the Fox and Hounds Inn, keeping L beyond it, past Danby Tennis Club. Where the road swings L, keep ahead on a public bridleway between gorse bushes, uphill onto Ainthorpe Rigg.

'Rigg', derived from Old Norse, is the local name given to a broad ridge. These moors are covered with standing stones, cairns and earthworks, and the northern end of Danby Rigg in particular is occupied by an ancient field

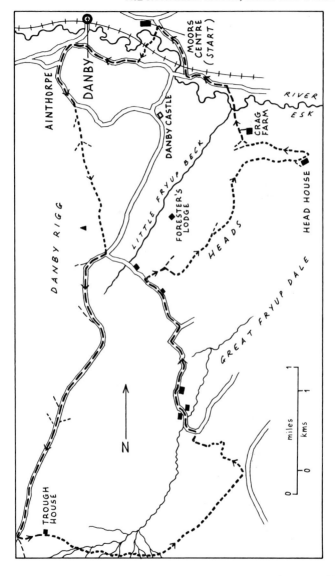

Standing stone on Danby Rigg

system and many stone-clearance heaps, burial cairns and funerary circles. One such feature is close by the path - a large standing stone surrounded by the remains of a large stone circle.

Continue over the moor top and down Crossley Side on a good track through bracken to a road junction at Slate Hill House. *(It is possible to short-cut the route here by taking the road opposite (SE) and rejoining the walk 200m beyond Stonebeck Gate Farm.)*

Turn R on the quiet road (New Way) climbing Danby Rigg, with good views down Little and Great Fryup Dales and over surrounding moorland as height is gained. In 2½ miles (4km), at a junction with 2 tracks L, take the L fork signed 'Public Bridleway' - this is the 'Cut Road' path round Great Fryup Head. *Trough House is clearly visible ahead and its substantial walls have provided a haven of shelter for many a walker on stormy days. It is normally used as a shooting cabin.*

Proceed ahead (E) in a shallow groove past numerous overgrown spoil heaps. The peaty path crosses many streams draining into the steep dale head and reaches a large cairn where a path (George Gap Causeway) drops L (N) into Great Fryup Dale. *There are rock scrambles below and the path forms a good escape route off the moor top.*

Climbing slightly to avoid the original track, now hopelessly boggy, our route rounds Great Fryup Head on any of several parallel trods which finally re-unite. Just before the road is reached on Glaisdale Rigg, a pile of stones marks the start of the descent into Great Fryup

Trough House, above Great Fryup Head

Dale, indistinct at first, but soon a boot's width. Follow this thin path carefully to a wall gate, whereafter it bears R more clearly down a groove, zig-zagging through bracken past rowan trees to a gate. Go through, and down an overgrown walled lane, turning R onto a metalled farm drive which joins the public road.

Turn L down to woods over the infant Great Fryup beck and continue on along the lane, past Wood End, Raven Hill and Slidney Beck farms, and uphill round a sharp R bend to a junction. Turn L (Signed 'Danby 4 miles') and climb to Fairy Cross Plain. *This seems to have been named, in the not-so-distant past, after a belief hereabouts in the 'little people'. Many years ago, witches' curses were wholly credible as the cause of mishaps and bad luck. Charms against spells included stones with a natural hole through them, horseshoes nailed to doors, and piercing a beast's heart with pins and roasting it at midnight. Amongst locally known witches were Nanny Howe of Kildale, Ann Grear of Guisborough, and Nanny Pearson of Goathland.*

Past Fairy Cross Plain cottage, walk downhill and in 250m, turn R into a walled green lane. Here begins the final leg along the side of Little Fryup Dale and back down to the River Esk. Go through a gate and turn R up towards a copse of Scots Pine, keeping L below it and along pleasant, brackeny hillside. The path climbs delightfully to the steep edge of Heads, overlooking the entire length of the dale.

When opposite the buildings of Forester's Lodge below, fork R on a

Danby Lodge Moors Centre

less distinct track away from the hill edge through bracken. This passes a marshy spring L and veers gradually L through more bracken to a wall gate above Crag Wood. Turn R into a field alongside the wall and follow it, then a fence, round R above Danby Crag to Head House. Just before the building, aim ½-L down to a wooden gate and walk along the bridleway outside the property's N wall. Immediately after a bridleway sign, turn L down across rough ground to join an earth track, turning L to reach a wall corner. Follow the wall (on its L), go through a gate and into tall bracken. *During the summer when bracken and undergrowth are at their densest, it is horses using these tracks and bridleways, rather than walkers, which keeps them open.*

Our way now enters Crag Wood. *It is an ancient, uncleared stretch of natural woodland containing all kinds of trees, including oak, birch, hazel, holly and other species; there are several almost magical glades. The way is paved too, possibly part of one of the old Pannier Ways which criss-cross the region.*

Emerging from the wood, we confront a conspicuous signpost. Keep ahead past a tree and down to a gate and track L of Crag Farm. This connects with a farm road which crosses the River Esk and leads to the main Esk valley road (Lawns Road), though itself not particularly busy. Turn L and walk back towards Danby, with good views to the S. Turning R under the railway, it is but a short stroll back to the Moors Centre. *(200m straight on, however, is Duck Bridge, one of the area's finest packhorse bridges and still able to take the weight of the occasional car over its sharp apex.)*

WALK 6   DANBY LODGE MOORS CENTRE - HOULSYKE - LEALHOLM MOOR - DANBY BEACON - MOORS CENTRE

7 miles (11.5km) - 3 hours - Easy terrain, but part exposed in bad weather.

For details on the Moors Centre, see Walk 5.

From the car park, walk down the road SE and in about 250m, turn L over a stile at a footpath sign and walk diagonally across the field to the top R corner, through a gate and along to Park House. *The name 'Park' crops up in many places in the Esk Valley, reminding us that wooded Deer Parks occupied large stretches of the valley floor from the 14th century, supplying game for the hunting gentry.*

Continue ahead through the farmyard and up to the minor road at a hairpin bend. Keep straight on past Oakley Side House and where the road begins to drop to Houlsyke village, turn L, cross a ladder stile and walk uphill to the R of a wall on this Concessionary Path. At the unfenced moor road near Oakley Walls Farm, turn R, gently descending above a maze of field enclosures bordering Eskdale (Oakley Walls).

Towards the end of the last Ice Age 12,000 years ago, ice from the encircling glaciers blocked meltwater channels at Kirkdale and Lealholm so that Eskdale and neighbouring Fryup and Danby dales were flooded to about the 700ft (213m) contour. The flat swathe of rich arable land now below us was laid down on the bed of this huge glacial lake.

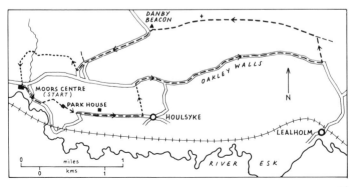

'Stump Cross' on Brown Rigg End

Soon after passing above Park Wood and Greystones Farm, the road reaches a R bend and begins to drop towards Lealholm. *(Walkers wishing to visit Lealholm village, or to return to Danby by train can turn R here to Lealholmside and on down to the valley bottom. To resume this walk entails a climb back up of some 300ft (90m). Lealholm, however, is worth the effort! A bridge and stepping stones span the Esk, here a wide, babbling river overhung by trees. There are picnic areas, a tea room, inn, shops and village green opposite a generous car park. On the wall of the Wesleyan Chapel near the stepping stones are marked the flood levels of 1840 and 1930. Elsewhere can be found 3 drinking fountains, no longer in use but built in 1904 when piped water finally superceded the supply from local springs.)*

Back at the moor top road bend, our route turns up a good stony track (N) at the bend sign. In 500m, turn L at a T-junction near Stick-i'-th'-Mire Bog and stride out on the firm surface across heather moor with views L of Upper Glaisdale and Great Fryup Dale.

At Brown Rigg End, to the R of the track after a stretch of gradual ascent, stands Stump Cross. Despite being only a broken stone pillar in a socketed base, its presence and obvious antiquity draws one's attention magnetically; those who have seen 'Fat Betty' on the moors to the south-west will notice a striking similarity.

The tall marker post on Danby Beacon acts as a focal point as the moor levels off to this the highest spot around, at just under 1000ft (299m). *In clear visibility, views extend from the tumulus and trig. points in all directions: west to Kildale, east to Goathland, south to the high moors above the Fryup Dales and, perhaps more excitingly, north over Scaling Dam Reservoir and the busy Whitby-Guisborough road to Tees-side.*

Leave the Beacon SW along the moor road for nearly a mile (1.5km) past many mounds from 18th and 19th century coal workings, and keep straight on (R) at a fork. In 200m, take a footpath sharp R and follow this downhill to the R of a wall. This swings L and leads to Clitherbeck, which is crossed, thereafter bearing ½-L uphill. Pass through the field gate into a wood, now walking S downhill back to the Moors Centre.

NOTE: A number of short family walks in and around the Esk Valley have been devised and waymarked by the North York Moors National Park; many start from the Moors Centre, Danby. They are explained in an excellent series of leaflets under the generic title of *Waymark Walks* which contain not only sketch maps and route directions, but also interesting additional information to add colour to your outing. Obtainable from local information centres or direct from The North York Moors Information Service, The Old Vicarage, Bondgate, Helmsley, York (tel. 0439 70657).

Duck Bridge, Danby

WALK 7   GLAISDALE VILLAGE - GLAISDALE RIGG - UPPER GLAISDALE - GLAISDALE VILLAGE

9½ miles (15km) - 4½ hours - Moderate; map reading useful in places.

Glaisdale village hugs a steep slope where Glaisdale meets Eskdale and is served by British Rail's Esk Valley line. In the mid-19th century, 3 blast-furnaces were in operation here, though the earliest recorded iron-ore smelting dates back to 1223. Sturdy, slate-roofed terraced houses were originally built for the miners. Today, Glaisdale's attraction lies in its riverside location, notably at Beggar's Bridge and East Arncliff Wood.

From the top of the village (The Green), walk SW past houses and through gates onto the lower slopes of Glaisdale Rigg *('Rigg' is an old Norse word for broad ridge).* Keep to the main track past an area of overgrown quarries to reach a water-filled hollow where other tracks converge. Fork R on a clear green way - the old Whitby road -unsuitable for motors but a splendid 1½ miles (2.5km) of firm going for the walker, climbing Glaisdale Rigg to its summit at 1069ft (326m) close to the metalled road; there are several inscribed stones along the way.

A short distance from the triangulation pillar, take an overgrown bridleway which leaves L (S) at an 'Unsuitable for Motors' sign. Cross a pipe connected by concrete inspection chambers and keep ahead towards a ruined barn (Red House) at a stand of trees. The path is narrow and likely to be overgrown with bracken, especially in high summer.

Turn L downhill with a wall on the R, through more bracken and a gate, down the next field and through 2 more gates then straight on to some trees, the wall now on the L. At the road, continue ahead over Hardhill Beck and past Yew Grange. *This charming lane, bordered with foxgloves, passes Hob Garth, a beautiful stone house with a very attractive garden.* Swinging L, we climb to Mountain Ash Farm, with its renovated cottages, and beyond the farm go through the middle of 3 gates, climbing a grassy, walled track and heading steeply up a field. Pass through a gate and bear R just below a TV aerial.

The route now follows a hollow groove, steadily mounting in a big zig-zag to open hillside. At the wall along Wintergill Plantation, the track is rather unclear: bear off R (S) over a grassy area between

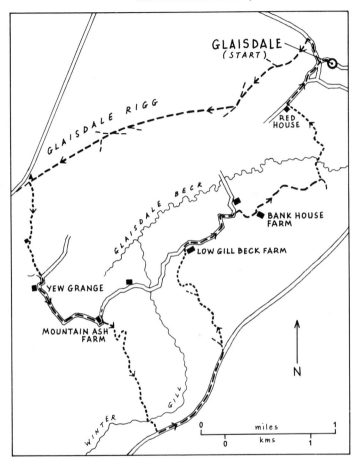

bracken, where the path re-establishes itself and crosses heather on Nab Rigg. Continue up to a gate in the wall now visible ahead. Now on open moorland, the pleasant track dips to cross Wintergill, a pretty spot, before reaching the high road from Rosedale to Eskdale.

Turn L along the tarmac to the far end of Wintergill Plantation, turning off down its E edge on a clear track for about 75m. At the corner of forest, fork R on a thinner path which passes between a cairn

49

Winter Gill

and an upright marker stone. *There are many such stones around Glaisdale Head, some bearing curious inscriptions from the early 18th century.*

The path now drops, with marvellous views over Glaisdale ahead. At a fork, go R (both paths are marked with blue arrows on rocks), through dense heather down by a groove to a wall and fence, continuing round to a gate. Go through and follow the fence and wall down through bracken to Low Gill Beck Farm. Cross some corrugated iron by a rowan tree and descend to the L of the farm by a duck pond and onto the public road.

Turn R and just before New House Farm, take a rough farm road R to Bank House Farm. Before reaching the buildings, go L on a stony track, through a gate, descending and swinging R through several field gates and over 2 streams. When a bend to the R more steeply uphill is reached, don't go up to the sheepfold but turn L downhill (no clear trod), aiming for an oak tree in a hedge. Keep ahead in the same direction and cross Glaisdale Beck at a good footbridge in the lowest part of the field.

Turn L here and climb on a paved way between hedges. At the top, go through a gate and turn L on another section of paved way. Follow this, with consistently good views of the dale, out into a lane to Red House. Turn R on the road and walk past St. Thomas' church back into Glaisdale village.

Paved causeways such as those just walked along are encountered frequently in the North York Moors region, though they do occur elsewhere in Britain too, notably the South Pennines. These lines of squared sandstone blocks, each averaging 18"-24" (46-60cm) in size, were for centuries the through-routes along which man and horse travelled over moor and dale alike. Without such solid causeways, teams of up to 40 pack ponies walking in single file would soon have become bogged down: many commodities were moved by packhorse from about the late 16th century onwards - wool, cloth, lime, ironstone, coal and charcoal, to name a few.

Over 150 miles (241km) of paved way is traceable in the North York Moors area, probably only a fraction of the original network. Usually their surface is worn hollow by the passage of hooves and feet over several centuries. New roads, along with culvert and wall building, have destroyed some examples, but many causeways still remain, sometimes buried under turf or vegetation but exposed in stretches. On footpaths carrying high densities of visitors today, new paving often represents the best way to prevent serious erosion.

WALK 8   RUNSWICK BAY - HINDERWELL - BORROWBY DALE - STAITHES - PORT MULGRAVE - RUNSWICK BAY

6½ miles (10.7km) - 3 to 3½ hours - Moderate; steep in places.

Runswick Bay, like all these northern coastal indentations, was once a deeper feature with more prominent headlands; glacial clays and gravels now soften its profile, the cliffs unstable and subject to rapid marine erosion. Fishing formed an important livelihood for centuries and until 1978 there was a lifeboat station here. In the mid-19th century, when jet ornaments were in high fashion, jet mines were worked to the east of the village. Nowadays, Runswick is mainly a tourist spot with good sands and a plethora of holiday homes.

From the clifftop car park, walk W along Hinderwell Lane (with pavement), past the Runswick Bay Hotel and Post Office. In about a mile, Hinderwell is entered at the World War I Memorial, where we turn R long the main street. In only 100m or so, turn L down a signed footpath between houses (marked, misleadingly, 'To Doctor's Surgery Only') and continue past Oakridge County Primary School, along by gardens, over a stile and along a field edge.

Another stile leads into Back Lane, a broad, earthy way between hedges, rather muddy if wet. Turn R along it, with views ahead of Boulby potash mine, a considerable industrial scar on the natural landscape. Where Back Lane turns R into Hinderwell village, go L over a stile and down a field by a hedged fence.

At the next stile and signpost, keep forward down a grassy bank to trees along Dales Beck. Cross the footbridge and go L up a steep little path through woods, emerging into an open field and turning R along its edge. At the field corner ahead, turn R into trees, then L on a path meandering very attractively through old deciduous woodland. Where a path comes up from the R, keep L and very soon after turn R onto a more prominent path at a post with yellow waymarks.

The woods are left behind at a metal gate, after which we keep ahead along a grassy bank and over a stile. The path widens to a track and drops through a caravan park. Turn R over the bridge and bear L onto a good made-up track with Dales Beck L. Keep L of 2 houses and turn R onto the public road at Dalehouse. Turn R uphill past the Fox and Hounds pub and R again at the Main A174 road.

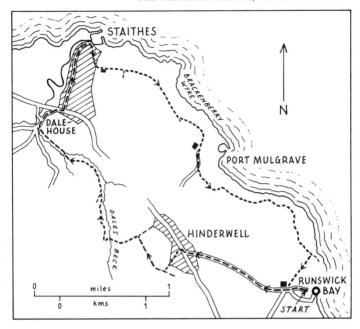

Glancing back, Boulby Mine is seen to its full extent. No-one will deny the commercial value of developing the potash field here, but the environmental impact of this huge industrial installation (the mine itself runs 3km out to sea, at a depth of 3600ft (1100m)) is a high price to pay. Although originally approved by the National Park Committee, future projects such as this may well be opposed.

A L turn to Staithes is signposted and our route follows it down to the charming little fishing village, over cobbles in the main street, past the 'Kipper and Gift Emporium' and out to the harbour.

Set in the narrow mouth of Roxby Beck, old Staithes huddles beneath high cliffs without room for gardens. Originally a fishing village but now largely given over to tourism, the lower town is unspoiled and full of interest. The 'Cod and Lobster' inn forms a focal point above a small sandy beach, while in Roxby Beck, the few remaining 'cobles' can be seen - local boats with high, sharp prows and wide amidships, built on Viking lines to deal with the often heavy surf. Staithes retains its seafaring traditions and is now an important lobster port. Before the 2 breakwaters were built, houses were prone to damage or destruction during storms.

Staithes

Prior to his maritime career, Captain Cook was apprenticed to a draper in the village. To commemorate the 250th anniversary of his birth, a Heritage Trail was set up in 1978, linking places in North Yorkshire associated with him. (See Walk 1).

From the W end of the beach, walk inland up a cul-de-sac, past Captain Cook's cottage and up steps, turning L onto the cliff path signed 'Cleveland Way'. Beyond modern farm buildings, the way is clear ahead, over stiles and through fields, some distance away from the cliff edge. Go steeply uphill over pasture, taking the R of 2 trods to a stile and signpost at the top.

The next 500m offer superb viewpoints, and at low tide vast rock platforms are uncovered on the shore below, Brackenberry Wyke being a superb example. The cliff path reaches the road at Port Mulgrave. *Once busy with iron-ore brought in by rope-hauled railway wagons from mines around Boulby, but now rather forlorn, its jetty is half derelict and the little harbour hopelessly choked with mud and stones.*

Where the road bends R at the Ship Inn sign, turn L along the coast path by a bench. Mostly arable fields are passed, and a steep, slippery down and up over Rosedale Wyke (waterfall) is negotiated before a ladder stile is crossed and there are more marvellous clifftop views to enjoy.

Old fencing below at Lingrow Cliffs bears witness to this coast's propensity for slipping into the sea; indeed, the entire original village of Runswick disappeared one fateful night in 1664. Soon, Runswick Bay is in view as the path twists along outside fields. Turn R at a stile and sign, walk along a field edge, over a stile and ahead between hedge and fence, to reach the Runswick Bay Hotel, turning L back to the car park.

WALK 9   RUNSWICK BAY - KETTLENESS -
ROMAN SIGNAL STATION -
DISMANTLED RAILWAY -
RUNSWICK BANK TOP & BAY

6 miles (9.5km) - 3 hours - Moderate.

Runswick Bay village, nestling below high cliffs, contains a number of interesting old buildings dating from times when its population as a fishing community was considerably greater than the present 40 or so inhabitants: much of Runswick is now devoted to tourism.

NOTE: This walk, from the beach car park, cannot be started until the tide is partly out. At high water, especially in rough weather, the beach top is often covered and any attempt to force a way along the muddy and eroded cliffs behind Runswick Sands is both dangerous and futile, despite myriad overgrown tracks.

Walk along the sands, past Runswick Bay Sailing Club and the first large cliff containing Hob Holes. *Though somewhat silted up and overgrown, the caves wherein resided a hob, or goblin, reputed to cure whooping cough, can still be seen: they were extended by jet mining activity in the 19th century.*

Beyond Hob Holes, take a path R up a distinctive stream valley,

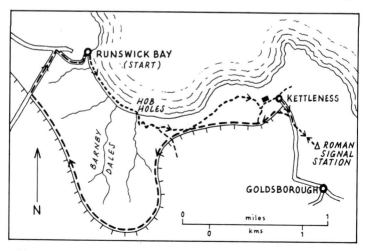

Runswick Bay

following its bed, crossing it on a footbridge and climbing steep steps up its L bank. *The stiff ascent is rewarded by very good views of the bay. Along the grassy cliff edge above old alum workings, hawthorn hedges have been sculpted by wind action.*

Following the clear cliff path (we are on the Cleveland Way), cross Cat Beck, pass a white chalet and go through Kettleness Farm yard. (If full of cows, go round the seaward side!) At the road end, turn R, and just before a derelict chapel on the L, go through a gate and over a stile, cutting diagonally across a field and aiming to the L of some ruined farm buildings. Another stile leads to the Roman Signal Station, 'Scratch Alley'.

The grassy mound we see today once supported a high timber or stone lookout tower, one of a chain used to warn of possible invasion from the North Sea, and to communicate other information about shipping during the 4th century A.D. Other towers were situated at Huntcliffe (near Saltburn), Goldsborough (near Whitby), Ravenscar, Scarborough and Filey Brigg. Even minus the superstructure, views from the mound are commanding, from Boulby Cliff in the north-west to Whitby Abbey in the south-east. Retrace steps towards Kettleness and turn L along the cinder track bed of the old Yorkshire Coast railway.

On the left are hillocks and hollows of the Kettleness Ironstone Mine. None of the coastal seams south-east of Staithes were of good enough quality

57

to be worked for very long. In any case, winter storms made transportation by sea difficult: inland mines served by a growing railway network were more important during the mid-19th century when the industry was at its height, meeting demand for iron to build ships, railways and for general engineering.

Where the coast path is met, the outward route presents a short-cut back to Runswick Bay if required (but note the state of the tide). *Although the railway track bed is not an official right-of-way, it is frequently walked and provides a pleasant, easy stroll back to the start.*

Beyond a bridge, the track swings inland, skirting a vast area of scrubby wasteland and the deep, wooded valley of Barnby Dales. *Earlier this century, these slopes were occupied by holiday chalets. Landslip and neglect have wrecked the area and only a few ruins remain amidst impenetrable undergrowth.*

There are many wild flowers along the way and the view ahead is dominated by Boulby Potash Mine and Boulby Cliff, the latter rising to 699ft (213m) at Rockcliff Beacon. Curving round R (NW) and passing through gates, we reach the public road at Runswick Bank Top. Turn R and walk along to Runswick Bay Hotel, turning R again down the steep road to the bottom car park.

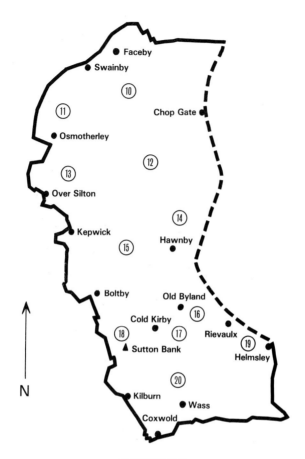

CHAPTER 2

BILSDALE, THE HAMBLETON HILLS
AND WESTERN MOORS

Bounded to the east by Bilsdale and Ryedale, and to the west by the sudden escarpment beyond which the Vale of Mowbray stretches away for over 20 miles (32km) to the Pennine foothills, this chapter contains two distinctive areas.

First, to the south of Hawnby, are the Hambleton Hills which form a gentle dip slope whose soil supports arable farming up to the 1000ft (305m) contour. It is a landscape of large fields and scattered settlements, punctuated here and there by forestry plantations. The escarpment itself is of unusual interest to the walker, providing many miles of spectacular views and good firm going: amongst other walks, it is the route taken by the Cleveland Way. Two exceptionally fine ecclesiastical ruins - Rievaulx and Byland Abbeys - share the south-east corner with the ancient market town of Helmsley.

The second area, north of Hawnby, is a transition to wilder, higher moorland, largely heather covered and, apart from a road between Osmotherley and Hawnby, accessible only on foot, and even then not widely. The Cleveland Hills scarp slope, often heavily afforested, continues as a prominent feature, offering good varied walks and a succession of villages at its foot.

With the exception of the A170 between Thirsk and Pickering, this chunk of the National Park is crossed west to east only by a few minor roads, the main thoroughfares being the A19 trunk road to the west, and the B1257 down Bilsdale. Thirsk and Battersby Junction are the nearest railway stations.

The Walks

Starting in Scugdale, Walk 10 climbs open moor on good tracks to Carlton Bank, with its Gliding Club airstrip, returning along the well used escarpment path over Live Moor. From the quiet market town of Osmotherley, Walk 11 makes a shorter circuit, past the start of the famous Lyke Wake Walk on Scarth Wood Moor and back through South Wood, with an optional extension to Mount Grace Priory, the impressive remains of a Carthusian monastery. Walk 12 traverses wild and remote moors, on good tracks, at the heart of the Cleveland Hills, reaching a Bronze Age burial mound (Green Howe) and good viewpoint.

Threading through forest on the moor edge, Walk 13 climbs diminutive Oak Dale above Osmotherley to take an exciting line over Black Hambleton and along the old Drove Road, before dropping to Kepwick and a country lane back to Nether Silton. Walk 14 encircles Hawnby and Easterside Hills, hogbacks smoothed by glacial action. Starting from Hawnby church, Walk 15 climbs to the top of the Hambleton Hills past fields sown with arable crops, takes a short section of the Drove Road, then heads down secretive Stoney Gill

Hole, skirting Coomb Hill.

The marvellous ruins of Rievaulx Abbey form a fulcrum for Walk 16, which first follows the River Rye upstream before veering off to Old Byland and thence by field paths to Nettledale and lanes back to Rievaulx. Walk 17 starts and finishes at Scawton's village pub and includes a broad slice of rural countryside, through Cold Kirby and on out-of-the-way woodland paths above Kilburn.

Sutton Bank Information Centre makes a fitting base for Walk 18 which explores the escarpment from above and below, extending south to the Kilburn White Horse and north beyond Gormire Lake. Helmsley is the National Park's administrative home and is also a popular tourist spot. From the ancient market cross, Walk 19 uses easy field paths, woodland tracks and country lanes to reach Rievaulx Abbey, with a return either by bus or through the Duncombe Estate. A climb through delightful woods from Wass hamlet leads to the Mount Snever tower, from where Walk 20 continues through Oldstead and on field paths to the stately ruins of Byland Abbey. Undulating farmland leads circuitously back to Wass.

Sessile Oak

WALK 10 HUTHWAITE GREEN - SCUGDALE - CARLTON MOOR - LIVE MOOR - HUTHWAITE GREEN

6½ miles (10.5km) - 3 to 4 hours - Moderate.

Ironstone mining on the flanks of Whorlton Moor and in Scugdale during the latter half of the 19th century has given way to a far more peaceful industry - that of forestry, which has transformed much of the Cleveland Hills' northern escarpment.

The walk begins at Huthwaite Green, a tiny hamlet on a back road SE of Swainby. There is some parking space in the vicinity of a telephone box, but care is needed to avoid inconveniencing passing traffic.

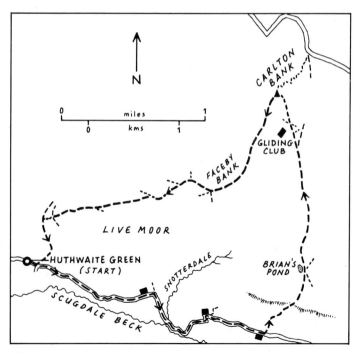

View north from Carlton Bank

Walk SE along the narrow road up Scugdale, with views ahead of Whorlton Moor and the dale's upper reaches. Continue round the sharp R turn beyond Sparrow Hall, dropping to cross Snotterdale Beck (from a branch of Scugdale) at a ford. A L turn and a hairpin bend at Raikes Farm lead on beneath the line of Barker's Crags to Scugdale Hall.

Here we turn L (NE) on a track up through brackeny fields to a steep break in Barker's Crags, whereafter the way is almost level to Brian's Pond, where a path comes in from the R. *Views hereon are excellent: to the south-east Barker's Ridge leads to Green Howe (see Walk 12), to the west is Raisdale, a branch of Bilsdale, while farther to the north-east, between Cringle and Cold Moors, stands Captain Cook's Monument on Easby Moor.*

Continue climbing onto Whorlton Moor on a clear track towards Carlton Bank Gliding Club. A 'Gliding Field - Beware of Flying Operations' notice is to be heeded on busy flying days! Still on the broad, rutted track, fork R and contour round the moor edge to approach the R-hand (E) side of the Gliding Club, heading for the OS pillar on Carlton Bank (avoid walking across the runway).

The extensive alum workings on Carlton Bank, closed in 1771, have in recent years degenerated into a dusty (or muddy) desert under the onslaught of trail bikes: if an area such as this is sacrificed to that sport, it is only to be hoped that other, less accessible, moorland sites escape, since the visual and audial pollution is a blight to the walker. In fact, Carlton Bank is often buzzing with activity on fine weekends; gliding, hang-gliding, mountain-bikers, joggers and walkers on the very popular escarpment path all adding to the over-use problem.

So it may be with some relief that we now turn L (SW) from the OS pillar (a fine viewpoint at 1338ft - 408m) on a bare, eroded track along the scarp, ignoring paths off L and R. Since we are on the routing of numerous well known walks, including the Cleveland Way, Lyke Wake Walk and Coast to Coast Walk, there can be no doubting the path, which makes a pale, stony scar above Faceby Bank and over the N flank of Live Moor. Several cairns and boundary stones are passed before a stepped slope is descended through a conifer plantation fire-break.

At the bottom, turn L on a bridleway skirting the edge of Live Moor Plantation, noticing the overgrown mounds nearby which date from the days when the ironstone industry thrived hereabouts. The track veers R and leads back down to the road at Huthwaite Green.

WALK 11   OSMOTHERLEY - SHEEPWASH
CAR PARK - SCARTH NICK
BEACON HILL - SOUTH WOOD -
OSMOTHERLEY

5½ miles (8.5km) - 2½ to 3 hours - Easy to Moderate.

Testimony to its own antiquity, Osmotherley's church still contains fragments of Saxon crosses and a 10th century 'hogsback' stone in the porch. As the crow flies, it is not far to industrial Teesside, and the busy A19 is only a mile away to the west, yet Osmotherley seems almost quintessentially rural. Once an important market town, it is now a rather sleepy, old-fashioned village, well visited by holidaymakers and walkers. The moor road over to Hawnby and Ryedale gives easy access to much fine walking, including Black Hambleton and the Drove Road (see Walk 13).

This route starts from Osmotherley's ancient stone market cross. *(Just opposite, down a narrow alleyway, stands one of England's earliest non-conformists chapels, dating from 1754.)*

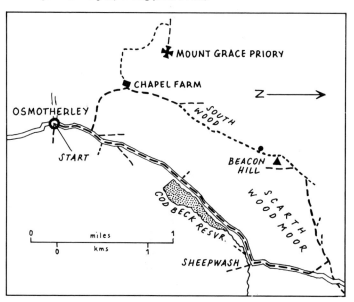

In South Wood, above Osmotherley

Walk N up past the General Store and the campsite (below R), straight ahead along Quarry Lane, which usually carries only light traffic.

At the far end of Cod Beck Reservoir is a large picnic and car parking area known as Sheepwash - *a favourite spot for visitors in the summer and the starting point for the Lyke Wake and Shepherds' Round challenge walks. The track going south - a continuation of the road's line - is the Hambleton Drove Road, used by the White Rose Walk.*

Continue N along the tarmac to Scarth Nick, a narrow notch in the escarpment created by glacial meltwater towards the end of the last Ice Age. Here, the main walking thoroughfare along the escarpment crosses from west to east; before the road drops steeply to the agricultural plain, we turn L at a cattle grid, short-cutting a sharp corner, and climb the broad track onto Scarth Wood Moor.

Pass through a gate and proceed ahead by a wall above Arncliffe Wood to the OS pillar on Beacon Hill (982ft - 299m), traditional start of the Lyke Wake Walk. *200m beyond, a forest of aerials and dishes bristles from British Telecom's Transmitting Station, but long before the age of telecommunications, this was an important signal station, as the name Beacon Hill implies. Despite the forestry plantation, views are far-reaching in clear weather, over the A19 and across the Vale of Mowbray to the distant Pennines.*

The waymarked path (Cleveland Way) now dips into South Wood, emerging to join a cart track beyond a gate at the tree edge. This leads easily down to Chapel Farm, whence a paved way leads west, then north, to Mount Grace Priory (an optional extension to this walk, or a separate excursion from Osmotherley).

Built in the early 15th century, the buildings housed Carthusian monks who lived here in solitude, though each had his own roomy cell and garden. The Dissolution of the Monasteries in 1539 left it open to the vagaries of weather and stone theft, but Mount Grace remains one of Britain's best preserved Carthusian foundations. The complex is now owned and cared for by the National Trust and is open to the public.

Pass to the L of Chapel Farm and follow Rueberry Lane round E, past private residences back to the road. Turn R down to Osmotherley's market cross.

Emperor Moth

WALK 12   SCOTLAND FARM - COW RIDGE - HEAD HOUSE - GREEN HOWE - ARNSGILL RIDGE - LOW COTE FARM - SCOTLAND FARM

8½ miles (14km) - 3½ hours - Easy terrain but exposed in bad weather.

There is limited car parking space off the Osmotherley-Hawnby road just above Scotland Farm; the turning is signed 'Footpath to Chop Gate'. Where the track bends down R to Scotland Farm, go through the gate ahead (N) and out onto a good sandy track over heather moor. *More than any other, this walk is dominated by the tall aerial mast of Bilsdale Transmitting Station to the NE. During August and early September, beehives are put on these moors and the busy background buzzing of bees, as well as the fragrant scent of heather blossom, becomes a familiar accompaniment to walks on the tops.*

Pass a tall cairn at Iron Howe and continue ahead, ignoring turns off L and R. Towards the valley head, our track veers sharply down L, with Head House now in view, and undulates along the valley side. Go through a gate, cross Arns Gill and climb to Head House. *Unlike so many abandoned hill farmhouses which soon succumb to the onslaught of weather or are used as rough barns, Head House is still intact. A notice on the front door requests visitors to keep it shut and the sheep out. The rooms inside may be bare, except for a bench or two, and the walls covered with graffiti, but there are fireplaces and in cold or stormy weather it would provide welcome shelter.*

Turn L (SW) from Head House, at first on level grass, then at a wooden post turn R (N) along a sandy track. (NOTE: If time is short or conditions poor, this detour to Green Howe and back can be omitted.) Ignore a faint path off L to grouse butts and walk ahead, ascending gently. Pass a track off L to Whorlton Moor *(the TV Relay Station above Osmotherley is just visible to the W)*, the way now a delightfully firm track across beautiful heather moorland. Green Howe tumulus has been a distant, nipple-like feature on the skyline but is now close at hand, topped by a boundary stone and reached along a clear track R.

In clear visibility, this is a marvellous viewpoint. L to R ahead are Whorlton Moor, Live Moor, Carlton Bank, Cringle Moor, Hasty Bank, Urra Moor and Bilsdale East Moor. The Cleveland Way runs along the northern escarpment from Live Moor to Urra Moor. Farther to the N lies

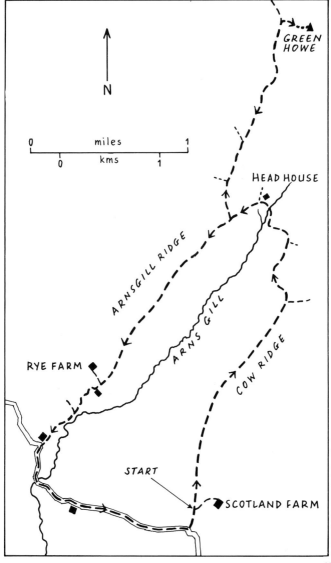

N

miles

0 ——————————————— 1

kms

0 ——————————————— 1

GREEN HOWE

HEAD HOUSE

ARNSGILL RIDGE

ARNS GILL

COW RIDGE

RYE FARM

START

SCOTLAND FARM

The track to Head House

the urban sprawl of Middlesborough.

Turn round and retrace steps to the wooden post SW of Head House. Turn R (SW) and walk along Arnsgill Ridge, the track slowly descending to a gate in the intake wall. Pass through and down a walled field edge. Soon a farm road is reached just past a barn at Hill End Farm; turn R and follow it as it winds down to a gate and walkers' signpost to Chop Gate. Here turn L, down and up to Low Cote Farm where the public road is reached. Go L downhill, veering L at Wheat Beck and climbing past Plane Tree Farm and Birk Wood back to the start above Scotland Farm.

WALK 13   NETHER SILTON - OVER SILTON -
THIMBLEBY BANK - OAK DALE -
BLACK HAMBLETON AND THE DROVE
ROAD - GALLOW HILL - KEPWICK -
NETHER SILTON

---

*12 miles (19km) - 5 to 6 hours - Moderate but more
strenuous and exposed in one or two places in bad
weather.*

*There is roadside parking at Nether Silton (south of Osmotherley) and at its
village pub.*

Walk E from the village and in 300m, turn L along Kirk Ings Lane.
Keep L at a fork and continue along this little used road to Over
Silton. Turn R up a cul-de-sac in the village, past a telephone box and
enter Forestry Commission land on a bridleway to Thimbleby. Ignore
a track R and pass a gate. At a junction, take the L of 3 tracks, an
earthy one climbing up and round in forest. Fork R, still in forest, as
the track climbs, veering R to become due N. Extensive use by horses
has churned up the surface, but even if very muddy after rain, the
edges are walkable on.

At the next fork, go L slightly downhill, eventually rising and
reaching open views to the L above a recently felled area - very
welcome after a section enclosed by trees. *Thimbleby appears below,
Osmotherley to the north, while away to the west the Vale of Mowbray
stretches for over 20 miles (32km).*

From the next track junction, turn L on a less distinct, rather
marshy ride which soon turns into a pleasant path, narrowing through
bracken and rowan before climbing sharply up over a rocky outcrop.
Emerging at a good forest track, there is a sign 'Landowners welcome
caring walkers' which is a vast improvement on the 'Private-Keep
Out' mentality. Turn L to reach open moor at a fence.

Our route now drops L inside the fence, over a stile R, and out
across heather and grass moorland. At the time of writing, the path is
waymarked by blue flags on poles - a method needing regular
attention as the weather takes its toll. Cross a stile and pass through a
small copse to another stile over a wall. The delightful contouring path
enters Big Wood and swings R through bracken, Black Hambleton
suddenly in view ahead. It then veers L, dropping into woods,

71

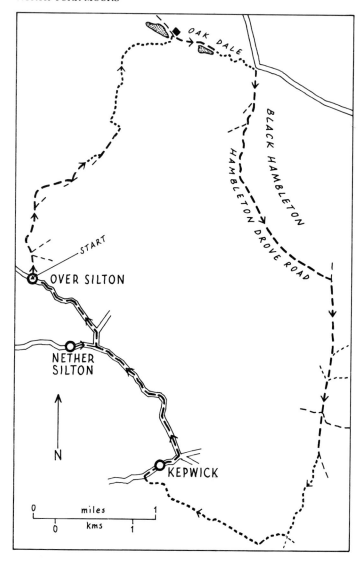

OAK DALE

BLACK HAMBLETON

HAMBLETON DROVE ROAD

START

OVER SILTON

NETHER SILTON

N

KEPWICK

| 0 | miles | 1 |
| 0 | kms | 1 |

through heather then more steeply down in trees to cross a wooden footbridge over Oakdale Beck. Aim to the L of Oak Dale ruin and turn R up a firm track, now on the Cleveland Way (though in the opposite direction to normal).

Cross a ladder stile and walk alongside Yorkshire Water Authority's reservoir, one of two in Oak Dale. A footbridge in a copse at the E end leads over Jenny Brewster's Gill, the route thereafter climbing brackeny hillside and provided with duckboarding over a marshy section. There is a steep climb to the Osmotherley-Hawnby road at a bend, where we turn off R on a rough track mounting the W flanks of Black Hambleton.

The Hambleton Drove Road, along which we shall walk for the next 3 miles (5km), enters the National Park from the north and climbs from Scarth Nick onto Osmotherley Moor. From here, it runs south along the escarpment, down to Oldstead and Coxwold and out of the Park on its long course to the old markets which once served the expanding industrial centres of population before an adequate road and rail network had become established. Sheep and cattle were driven south from Scotland and the Outer Isles, grazing along the way and tended by a hardy breed of drovers who had to deal with adverse weather, attempts to steal stock, and disease, as well as negotiate best selling prices. Pack horses also used the Drove Road, carrying lime, iron and other commodities. Carriage, coach and wagon transport increasingly turned to the new turnpike roads, but drovers continued to use the rough, unmade, toll-free tracks, saving money and time.

Our route crosses 2 stiles and climbs the rutted, stony Drove Road along the edge of forest. *(There is an easy short-cut from here back to Nether Silton - a distance of about 1¾ miles (3km) - should weather or circumstances dictate. Turn off R at a Forestry gate signed 'Bridleway to Nether Silton'. This meets a forest road, down which turn L. Ignore a R turning, pass Silton picnic area and continue ahead onto a metalled road past Moor House. At a T-junction, turn L and in 200m turn R into Nether Silton.)*

The summit of Black Hambleton - 1309ft (399m) - is easily reached up to the L, but at a cairn the track itself is scarcely any lower. Depending on conditions, views from here are as fine as from anywhere on the Hambleton Hills.

The Drove Road now levels off, with a high wall on the R: those of small stature have to make do with views where it has fallen down! After about ½ mile (800m), the track swings sharp R with the wall, by a junction with a track L signed 'Private'. *From here south, the Drove Road is exceptionally wide and grassy and is used for galloping horses.* Beyond some disused quarries L, pass through gates into and out of an

The Drove Road over Black Hambleton

enclosed section.

  Hereabouts once stood Limekiln House, an inn at the centre of the lime-burning and carrying trade: it catered for the thirsty quarrymen as well as passing drovers. Other inns along the Hambleton Drove Road were Chequers, now a farm and café on the Osmotherley-Hawnby road above Oak Dale; Dialstone Inn, also now a farmhouse just north of Sutton Bank; and the Hambleton Hotel on the A170 east of Sutton Bank - the only surviving hostelry.

  The stony old Kepwick Road crosses from west to east, but we continue ahead, wall to the R, still on the Cleveland Way. Pass a boundary stone L, then go through a gate in a wall marked 'Private' and through a gate in a fence. Now watch for a thin path leaving SW over flat ground. Follow it R of a conspicuous tumulus and drop down the scarp slope in a sunken groove towards a wall corner at Gallow Hill, a reminder of times when cattle thieves and highwaymen received rough justice. Go R through a gap in the wall and keep to the main path downhill, staying R of the wall down to a small gate.

Bracken gives way to heather as we continue down to the edge of Cowesby Wood, with good views R of Kepwick Hall in the sheltered hollow of Eller Beck. There are dwarf silver birch to the R, then heather and bilberry and bracken again as the path gradually veers R away from the wall. Head for a worn groove in the flank of Pen Hill, descending more steeply past wild rhododendrons and passing below Atlay Bank crags. Go through a gate and down a field to the road. Turn R through Kepwick village, L at a junction, and walk along quiet Bridge Beck Lane to the start at Nether Silton.

In a field behind the church stands a stone pillar bearing a mysterious rhyme which no-one has been able to decipher - it is worth a peep to attempt to solve the enigma.

Bracken

WALK 14 HAWNBY - HAWNBY HILL - CROW NEST
- EASTERSIDE HILL - WASS HOUSE
-HAWNBY

5 miles (8km) - 2½ hours - Moderate

There is limited parking in upper Hawnby village and at Hawnby Hotel (bar food, accommodation).

From the hotel, walk W along the road and opposite Manor Farm turn R through a gate and up a farm track. As the track curves on, there are good views of Hawnby Hill's stony western slopes and of wooded Coomb Hill to the W. Keep on the main track, through a gate

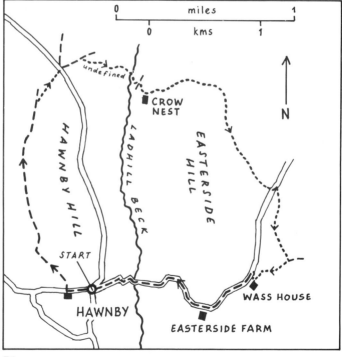

Hawnby Hill from ruined Crow Nest Farm

and alongside a plantation edge, through another gate and past Hill End House. *Views broaden out again as the N end of Hawnby Hill is skirted, from this angle a steep hump, a hogback almost identical in size and shape to nearby Easterside Hill.*

At a corner of wire fence where the track has become greener, take a thin path over grass veering ½-R and aiming, in clear visibility at least, to the R of the Bilsdale transmitting mast on the moors ahead. The path leads round above a small conifer plantation to the Hawnby-Osmotherley road. Turn L over a cattle grid and immediately R at a track intersection.

Walk down the track and just beyond a wooden post, fork R across heather to a double stile at a field angle (not to a gate R). Cross into marshy pasture, keeping well L and aiming towards the L end of Easterside Hill's ridge. Go down a groove, through a wall gap and low trees and head down towards a 'V' of pasture in the wooded valley of Ladhill Beck. Follow an old wall down R, and at the bottom turn R into trees, over a wooden footbridge and out alongside another old wall to its corner. Here turn uphill, following it to a gap R and crossing an earthy farm track. The path now slants up L towards trees and reaches the derelict Crow Nest Farm.

Pass through a small gate L and walk up the edge of heather moor by a good wall, making sure to pause and look back at Hawnby Hill, seen well from here. *A wide panorama has opened out to the north-west over Arden Great Moor and Snilesworth Moor and north to the moors flanking Bilsdale.* Follow the wall up to its highest point adjacent to Pepper Hill, the northern end of Easterside Hill, and continue round through heather, now on the E flanks with good views over Bilsdale. *The transition is clear to see from rough heather moor grazed by sheep, to fields, trees and farmsteads below the intake wall.*

Pass a diversion sign avoiding an overgrown quarry as the very pleasant path contours along, half-way up Easterside Hill. After about 300m, it descends gently, crosses a stile and a small paddock to reach Easterside Lane. Walk L for 60m, then cross a stile R, slanting back below the road. Pass a ruin, R, and follow the bottom field edge to a stile and gate, continuing ahead over pasture.

Where an earth track joins from the L, turn R through a gate and up the field edge by a fence towards trees. When level with Wass House, cross a stile L, walk towards the buildings and turn R between sheds, up to an old track. Turn R up it, doubling back L at a wire fence and reaching the road again at a gate.

Turn L and walk back to Hawnby village (about 1 mile, 1.5km). *Just past Easterside Farm, the whole length of Hawnby Hill comes into view, its narrow, north-south profile fashioned by glacial action during the last Ice Age.* The lane drops and climbs very steeply at Ladhill Beck before joining the Osmotherley road near a telephone box in the village. Apart from Hawnby Hotel, there are no other shops or amenities in the upper village.

WALK 15 HAWNBY CHURCH - SUNNYBANK FARM
- HAMBLETON DROVE ROAD - KEPWICK
OLD ROAD - STONEY GILL HOLE -
HAWNBY CHURCH

8 miles (13km) - 3½ to 4 hours - Moderate

All Saints, Hawnby, stands in a tranquil wooded setting by the River Rye, 750m west of the village. Inside, an extract from the Yorkshire Herald of Monday October 23rd, 1916, declares Hawnby's 'Proud Record of a Moorland Parish' - some 40 soldiers from the locality had already died in battle and presumably the toll was even heavier by the end of World War I.

Walk along the road towards lower Hawnby for about 100m, then cross the River Rye on the elegant little Dalicar Bridge. Turn R alongside the river, following a wire fence, then turn L up by a small tributary stream. Cross a stile and an old green track, keeping straight up alongside the stream, crossing to its R side then turning L through a gate and up to a farm track from Sunnybank Farm, now only 100m away L.

Turn R uphill past copses and thickets, with North Bank Wood R. Ignore a L fork and pass through a gate, with superb, wide views opening out all round. The route now passes L of wind-damaged barns used for sheltering beef cattle in winter - High Buildings - and continues forward on a good field track. At a metal gate and small ruin, keep straight on, the track becoming more overgrown and stony from field clearance. At the next gate, the path emerges onto open moor.

Alkaline soil conditions which allow arable farming in the previous fields so high up (1000ft, 300m) are due to outcropping of the Hambleton Oolite. Ahead, the moor landscape is one of heather and grasses, dotted with solitary trees and the occasional hard edges of plantations.

Proceed ahead ½-L across the top of a narrow valley and branch L along a clear track past the top corner of Sunny Bank Wood. At the next path intersection, turn R and in 600m R again along the Hambleton Drove Road.

This ancient drove road is one of a system of routes established in medieval times and used widely for moving animals before an efficient rail and road network existed. Cattle and sheep were driven south, grazing along the way, from as far afield as Scotland and the Outer Isles to markets in rapidly expanding industrial centres of population. Drovers themselves were

79

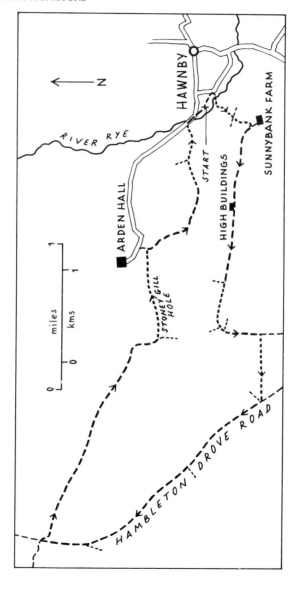

All Saints, Hawnby

a hardy breed, living in the open for months at a time and having to contend with all weathers, as well as protect their charges from sheep and cattle stealers. On the west flank of Black Hambleton, the drove road runs at an altitude of 1250ft (381m) and for much of its course along the Hambleton Hills it is a broad way, flanked by walls and old boundary stones and giving good, firm walking.

Just over ½ mile (800m) after leaving the corner of a conifer forest, pass through gates in fence and wall and pass a boundary stone R. This is also the Cleveland Way and follows a wall on the L to where a stony track crosses at right angles. Here turn R on the old Kepwick Road which veers L (E) across Little Moor. When the track drops to the edge of Thorodale Wood (after about 1¼ miles, 2km), take another track off R which comes down round to a wooden gate at the top of Stoney Gill Hole, a little dry valley.

Go down this tiny, secret dale, overgrown in summer with nettles and bracken and stony underfoot. Beyond a spring, the valley widens into open pasture, with symmetrical, wooded Coomb Hill directly ahead. *Arden Hall, out of sight but only 200m away over the ridge L, is a mainly 17th century building on the site of a 12th century nunnery.* Turn R onto a firm cart-track, ignoring a gate L into Nag's Head Wood which instead we skirt round in the delightful valley of Dalicar Brook, often alive with pheasants.

Past a gate, the track becomes rougher and undulates through cattle pasture. Where it bends sharp L uphill, go through the gate ahead and down a sunken way alongside Carr Woods. Pass through another gate and keep ahead to a telegraph pole and down to the road at Church Bridge *(parking space for 1 vehicle).*Cross the bridge and turn R down Hawnby's church walk and back to the start past a veritable forest of sandstone tombstones.

Curlew

WALK 16 RIEVAULX ABBEY - RYEDALE - OLD BYLAND - RIEVAULX BRIDGE

6½ miles (10.5km) - 2½ to 3 hours - Moderate

Starting from Rievaulx Abbey - a 'must' for any visitor to the North York Moors National Park - this route combines riverside and woodland walking with a visit to the quiet village of Old Byland. Some notes on Rievaulx Abbey appear first, since not only does it provide a fulcrum for the walk, setting the local landscape into context, but such information will be useful if a walk round the ruins is contemplated.

Lyrically situated at the junction of Ryedale and Nettledale, Rievaulx was northern England's first Cistercian monastery - 'a marvellous freedom from the tumult of the world' records St. Ailred in 1143. It was founded in 1132 and today is one of the region's finest ecclesiastical ruins, its great walls, soaring arches and graceful windows still hugely impressive. The choir, in particular, is a superb example of the 13th century stone mason's work.

Various outlying mounds and wall fragments testify to a far more extensive original site. Indeed, in its heyday, 140 monks and over 500 lay brothers (monks not in holy orders) lived and worked here, creating great wealth from sheep farming (at one time they owned 14,000 sheep), iron working, fishing and salt production on the coast. Towards the time of the Dissolution of the Monasteries, however, the house declined and fell into debt, and by 1536 only 22 monks remained. After 400 years of life, the site was eventually stripped for building stone and passed down to the Duncombe family: it was acquired by the State in 1918 and is now maintained by the Department of the Environment.

Because the site slopes westwards, the abbey was constructed on a north-south axis instead of the customary west-east. In its early days, there was no riverside land on this bank of the Rye which then flowed on the dale's east side. By agreement with Byland Abbey, who owned the west bank, new channels were cut, diverting the Rye to the west side of the dale on its present course.

From the abbey car-park, walk towards the red-roofed hamlet of Rievaulx, taking a path L off the road by a barn, signed 'Bow Bridge'. Passing through 2 gates, along between hedges and out onto riverside pasture, water-filled depressions may be spotted *(these old canals were used to transport materials during the building of Rievaulx Abbey).* Ashberry Woods clothe low hills opposite with dense deciduous

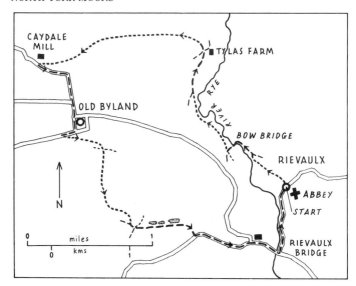

trees. Passing over 2 stiles, the River Rye is close by, flowing prettily over flat rocks beneath overhanging trees. Another stile leads onto a stony track, along which turn L to cross the old pack-horse Bow Bridge, surrounded by tall trees echoing with the quiet call of wood pigeon.

Over the bridge, take the signed path R to Hawnby, keeping to the lower grassy ledge between rampant bracken and cultivated fields. A stile provides access to a pleasant riverside wood, down through which the path twists pleasantly past oak, beech, hawthorn and alder. Conditions underfoot can be slippery as tree roots and little brooks are crossed, and where sheep have churned up the earth.

Emerging into the open, the route cuts across pasture at a river bend towards a track seen climbing ahead. *Crags up to the L are a disused quarry at the top of little Oxen Dale.* More bracken is encountered, then a gate climbed onto a metalled lane. Turn R to pass Tylas Farm; there are good retrospective views of pastoral Ryedale. At a track junction by a large tree, continue ahead through a gate and onto an earth track which soon becomes grassy and swings west.

Beyond a muddy stretch, the route climbs gently in thin deciduous woods leading to a level section through the conifers of Birk Bank plantation, with its wild raspberries and myrtle. Dropping gently

84

Rievaulx Abbey

through bracken, open slopes above a tributary of the Rye are reached, with Caydale Mill soon in view ahead.

Although signed 'Bridleway', a definite line is lost on rough, boggy pasture, but quickly regained above Caydale Mill, now converted to a private residence. At the road, turn sharp L, climbing steadily with lovely valley views, veering south at the top to join a bigger road. Ignoring a L turn, walk down into the sleepy village of Old Byland.

A settlement of neat cottages, farm buildings and paddocks, Old Byland is arranged timelessly round its grassy village green. Monks from Furness Abbey settled here before moving on to Byland Abbey. The quaint little Norman church is well worth looking at.

Turn R at the bottom road, past Valley View Farm (B & B). 50m beyond the County Council millstone sign, look for a small wooden gate L. The path slants back L, diagonally down and across a small nettle-choked valley - Hill Gill - before climbing out in the same direction to a gate by an old tree. Keep ahead across the stony track, through another gate by an electricity pole and along the edges of 2 fields, the second a long one.

Views over rolling countryside here on the Hambleton Hills are extensive and, behind, Old Byland is seen well. The distant aerial mast to the west is on Hambleton Down, not far from the escarpment edge.

At a gate and blue arrow, go L down through Callister Wood, past a sign for Nettledale and across a stream on a wooden footbridge. Keep ahead over a stile into a copse, ignoring a gate L and continuing to grassy levels and a bridge over a stream. *The Cleveland Way climbs R through plantations towards Cold Kirby.*

Turn L on a stony track (Bridge Road), past beautiful green ponds beneath Spring Wood. *Ducks frequent this sheltered backwater and in quiet weather, trees are reflected in the limpid surface.* Where track meets road, turn L and at a junction by picturesque Ashberry Farm, keep straight on, turning L at Rievaulx Bridge.

The wooded hillside ahead R largely conceals Rievaulx Terrace from this angle. It is, however, an extraordinary ½ mile of flowery woodland trail, owned by the National Trust and providing marvellous views of Rievaulx Abbey. Laid out in 1758 by Thomas Duncombe, there are mock Grecian temples at either end, the Ionic one furnished as a period dining room, with an exhibition in the basement of 18th century English landscape design. Overlooking one of Britain's most hauntingly evocative abbey ruins, Rievaulx Terrace is well worth the effort of a special visit. The entrance is found at the top of Rievaulx Bank off the B1257 road. (Open end-March to end-October)

The walk ends along a riverside lane, busy with cars and coaches in high season. At a bend, the abbey is suddenly revealed - an inspiring sight - and soon the car-park is reached, with its refreshments and access to the abbey ruins (open 11am to 5pm).

WALK 17 SCAWTON - NETTLE DALE - COLD KIRBY - HAMBLETON INN - COCKERDALE WOOD - SCAWTON

8½ miles (14km) - Easy terrain

There is roadside parking in Scawton village, and at the Hare Inn from where the walk begins. (Scawton lies between Rievaulx and Sutton Bank).

Walk down the road (NE) and at a sharp bend in 500m, take a track L to Stocking House. Watch carefully for a rather obscure path immediately off L which dives into Spring Wood: once through a

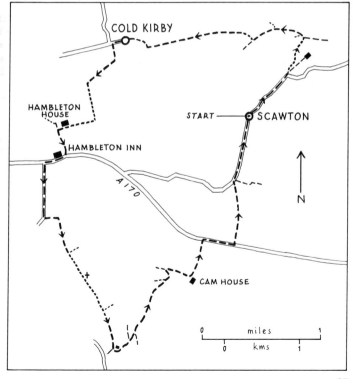

Arable farming on the Hambleton Hills

gate, it broadens out and drops to a footbridge where the Cleveland Way is joined.

Turn L along a surfaced forestry road, following Cleveland Way waymarks parallel to the stream. At Grass Keld Spring, bubbling out from beneath a tree, keep L on the track to the bottom of a dry valley - Flassen Dale - and climb R up a sunken way which can be overgrown. This leads out into Low Field Lane and thence into the village of Cold Kirby.

Pass through the village and turn L down a walled lane, at the end of which the Cleveland Way strikes ½-R along the old Cote Moor Road (now a track) across fields. Turn R at the edge of a conifer plantation and from Hambleton House stables go L on the metalled lane to reach the A170 near the Hambleton Hotel.

Turn R along the main road for 250m, then take to the minor road L signed White Horse Bank. Where it bears R at a crossroads, turn L on a stony track (unsuitable for motors) which turns sharp R and runs along the edge of woods. Ignore a track off L and proceed ahead on an earthy way, descending gently through trees. Emerging into the open, take a grassy path R by a curious chapel adorned with carved angels and a madonna. *This oddity is a memorial to three old boys of Ampleforth College killed during World War I.*

Go through a gate and drop down the forest edge on a pleasant, narrow bridleway, passing through another gate and along a field boundary with marvellous views over the lovely wooded country on the southern edge of these Hambleton Hills. Descending steadily, the path becomes a track.

By a white gate and house, turn L on an ascending track signed 'Leading to Cockerdale Farm' and at a green hut, continue straight ahead over a stile and into Great Cockerdale Wood. Ignore a turning off R and follow the broad track uphill. At a junction, keep R on the main track and after a short climb, turn R again. Pass through a gate out of the woods and walk along the track to ruined Cam House. Turn L just before the building and reach the A170 road, along which turn R for 500m, before taking a clear forestry track L. This emerges at a minor road and Scawton lies just ½ mile (800m) to the R.

Honey Bee

WALK 18   SUTTON BANK - KILBURN WHITE HORSE - SUTTON BANK - WHITESTONE CLIFF - TANG HALL - GORMIRE LAKE -SUTTON BANK

8 miles (13km) - 3½ to 4 hours - Easy to moderate

This walk forms a figure of 8 and can be started from any point or split into 2 separate parts. The Kilburn White Horse loop is 3 miles (5km) on easy terrain; the Gormire Lake loop is 5 miles (8km) over moderate terrain. The route avoids walking on the A170 which is often very busy.

Views from the outset of this walk are magnificent, not only of the escarpment cliffs and Gormire Lake, but west across the Vale of Mowbray, a vast, flat patchwork of fields and small settlements. In good visibility the Pennines will be glimpsed, notably Penhill and the gateway to Wensleydale.

From the Information Centre on Sutton Bank *(displays, books, refreshments, toilets: open 11am-5pm during holiday periods),* cross the A170 and take a broad grassy track S signed 'Kilburn White Horse'. Pass a junction at Castern Dike, where the Cleveland Way comes in L from the Hambleton Hotel and continue on a well walked, level path skirting Yorkshire Gliding Club's grassy airstrip.

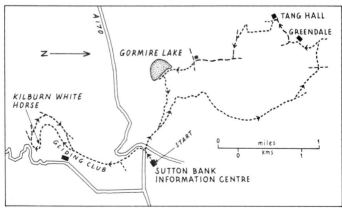

Sutton Bank Information Centre

Walkers are advised to keep an eye out for low-flying gliders and loose tow ropes on busy flying days. All along the scarp, prevailing westerly winds are pushed into up-currents of air by the curving 'bays' of cliff.

Go past a Forestry Commission sign at a path descending R and soon arrive at Roulston Scar, a conspicuous, jutting prow of rock and a superb vantage point.

Directly opposite, Hood Hill is crowned by Iron Age earthworks and a stand of deciduous trees above a cloak of conifers. Legend has it that Robin Hood fought his last battle here, while in earlier times, Druid priests held ritual sacrifices. Countryside to the south also swings into view - Kilburn village immediately below, with outlying hills and the Vale of Pickering L. In clear weather, York Minster can be spotted, 18 miles (29km) distant across the Vale of York.

A little farther on, the chalk head of Kilburn White Horse is reached; from here it is unrecognisable, its eye an island of turf. At a bench beyond the tail, descend steps R towards the car park below.

From this angle, the horse is simply a rough stony slope shored up with lateral timbers to prevent slippage; best views are from Carr Lane, just N of Kilburn village. A stone tablet reads: 'This figure was cut in 1857 on the initiative of Thomas Taylor, a native of Kilburn. In 1925, a restoration fund was subscribed by readers of the Yorkshire Evening Post and the residue of £100 was invested to provide for triennial grooming of the figure'.

In fact, the White Horse was marked out to Taylor's design by children from Kilburn school, under the supervision of their school master, John Hodgson: it was excavated by villagers. It measures 96m long by 70m wide and covers almost 2 acres. The White Horse Committee have restored its original shape, but its rather grey limestone base requires periodic dressing

Kilburn White Horse

with chalk to maintain whiteness. Visitors are requested to avoid walking over the surface.

From the car park, pass through a gate R and walk along a wide grassy track between conifers, ignoring a path L. In 200m, fork R. climbing gently then dropping to reach a track beneath the escarpment, along which turn R. *Views of the cliffs above trees and rampant rosebay willow herb are impressive - grey-gold crags split and fissured by the action of wind, rain and frost.*

At a fork, go R on an ancient, well-trod path climbing fairly steeply, with a handrail in places. *This is the 'Thief's Highway', once an escape route for highwaymen working the Hambleton Drove Road.* A wooden bench heralds the top, whence steps are retraced along the escarpment edge to Sutton Bank.

Gormire Lake is the only natural body of water in the North York Moors National Park and this next part of the walk passes above and alongside it, providing good impressions of its situation and character.

During the Great Ice Age some 20,000 years ago, a glacier hundreds of feet thick stretched from the moors across to the Pennines. Water escaping from glacial lakes to the north flowed down between the ice and the moor edge, excavating channels along the hillsides. When a glacial landslip subsequently blocked one such channel below Sutton Bank and Gormire Rigg, Gormire Lake was formed. It is fed from underwater springs, with an overflow to the east which mysteriously disappears. Surrounded by woodland of beech, ash and sycamore, the lake is both beautiful and

Gormire Lake

curious, a favourite haunt of botanists. Although circumventing paths are private, except for the one used on this walk, a special nature trail through Garbutt Wood has been set out, waymarked with numbered posts. Explanatory leaflets and guided tours are available from Sutton Bank Information Centre.

Cross the A170 and take the popular path signed 'Sutton Bank Trail' NW along the escarpment, ignoring a L fork. *Gormire Lake is seen at its best from this viewpoint. Soon a corner is turned, revealing the Hambleton Hills stretching N, and immediately below the undercut 'bays' of Whitestone Cliff, its rock belonging to the Upper Jurassic series dating back about 150 million years.*

The route ambles pleasantly alongside arable farmland above South Woods, for the time being on the Cleveland Way. Pass a sign R to the Hambleton Drove Road (about 400m E) and 100m before reaching a Cleveland Way signpost on top of the conspicuous tumulus ahead, (Windypit Hill Fort), watch out for a path slanting down L in a shallow gully. Follow this through a gate (blue arrow) and ahead between conifers. Continue alongside a wall on the R and swing down L by a ditch to cross a rough forestry track. Pass through a gate and out onto rough pasture, aiming towards deciduous trees below. Cross a stile and bear R down through bracken beneath old oak trees to a wall and signpost.

Turn sharp L (signed 'Tang Hall') through a gate and along a fence in bracken: in high summer, the path is rather overgrown. A gate leads R into open, gorsey pasture above Greendale Farm. Pass L of the buildings, through a gate and down a sunken earth lane in trees by a disused quarry. Just past a marshy area, turn R onto a track and then L along the surfaced farm track to Tang Hall.

Just by the farmhouse, turn L through a gate onto an old green track which swings L (ESE) across a field. Go through the gate and follow telegraph lines down a large pasture, with views now of South Woods, the escarpment 'scars' and the lower outlying hills.

At a gate by hawthorn bushes, turn R down by a hedge and at the bottom, go sharp L through a gate onto an earthy track. Pass a metal gate and turn L onto a surfaced farm track. Turn R at the next junction and walk gently uphill beneath beech trees to a house and gate. Continue ahead ½-L, signed 'Bridleway to Gormire'. In 50m, fork R over duckboarding through pleasant woodland along the E shore of Gormire Lake.

About half way along, by a 'No Fishing' sign on a tree, our route turns steeply L uphill to a fence and a 'Nature Reserve' sign. Continue on a good path, forking R at post no.10 *(a birch wood, with many ferns, wild raspberries, honeysuckle, bluebells and primroses in springtime)*. At post no.8, fork R again, the path now levelling off *(The Boulder Stone to the R has fallen away from the cliff above and is mainly sandstone with limestone nodules. Deer and other animals frequent the area.)* The path hereafter winds steadily up to the scarp edge at Sutton Brow, whereupon turn R back to Sutton Bank Information Centre and car park.

WALK 19 HELMSLEY - GRIFF LODGE - RIEVAULX - GRIFF LODGE - DUNCOMBE PARK - HELMSLEY

7 miles (11km) - 3 hours - Easy. Optional return to Helmsley by bus from the top of Rievaulx Bank

Helmsley is a picturesque Ryedale Market town, substantially given over to tourism and offering plenty of accommodation, including a youth hostel. Friday is market day and the square, with its ancient ornate cross, is surrounded by attractive buildings. There was a settlement here even in pre-Norman times, recorded as Elmslac in the Domesday Book.

Helmsley Castle, on the town's west side, was built in the 12th century by Robert de Roos, Lord of Helmsley, though many additions to the structure were made up to the 17th century. The keep is uniquely D-shaped. Following a seige by 1,000 troops under Sir Thomas Fairfax during the Civil War, the castle was rendered useless and subsequently yielded much of its stone for local building. What remains is now managed by the Department of the Environment and is still surprisingly impressive.

From Helmsley market square, walk west along Cleveland Way, an appropriately named lane for the start of this long distance route. Helmsley Castle is soon in view L, above manicured grassy banks, as the way proceeds along a stony, walled track. Cross a stile and walk L

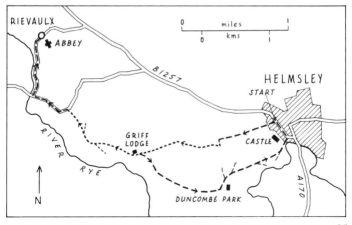

Market square, Helmsley

down a field edge, then R along the bottom and through 2 more fields separated by gates and ladder stiles.

A sign 'Cleveland Way and Rievaulx Abbey' points through a gate L and steeply down into an overgrown little valley, steps climbing the far side. Keep ahead alongside a wire fence past concrete foundations, all that remains of a World War II Polish Army camp. Pass through a rough paddock and out towards Griff Lodge. Cross its access track and continue ahead to a signpost, with open views L over Ryedale and back to Duncombe Park. The good path stays above Whinny Bank Wood at first, then descends gradually through it to a road bend at Ingdale Howl.

Turn L along the road for ½ mile (800m), turning R on a riverside lane to Rievaulx Abbey and village *(for notes about Rievaulx Abbey, refer to Walk 16)*. To return to Helmsley, either walk through Rievaulx village and up to the B1257, passsing the entrance to Rievaulx Terrace and catching a bus there; or retrace steps to Griff Lodge. Providing permission is obtained to pass through the grounds of Duncombe House (from the Estate Office near the gates in Helmsley), a variant is possible from here.

Instead of skirting the wall L from Griff Lodge, continue ahead on the main track, passing through trees and noting several more World War II concrete foundations. In 500m, bear L on a wide, surfaced track towards the large house, once the seat of the Earls of Feversham and now a private school. The route turns L in front of the building, then veers R, over a cattle grid and downhill to the main gates, with Helmsley Castle to the L. Turn L along the road back to the market square.

WALK 20   WASS - MOUNT SNEVER OBSERVATORY
- OLDSTEAD - BYLAND ABBEY - WASS

8½ miles (13.5km) - 4 to 4½ hours - Moderate

NB.   Although there are pub, Post Office and shop at Wass, parking is limited and care should be taken not to block private access.

From the crossroads where Wass Bank meets the Thirsk-Helmsley low road (bus route), turn L up a cul-de-sac, past attractive residences and through a gate up a broad stony track into lovely deciduous forest. Beyond a pond where the track veers R, with a gate to the L, climb the stile ahead into a field along the wood edge.

The path eventually bears R, uphill by an old wall through bracken. At a footpath sign L, cross the stile and take the R, upper, forest track which climbs steadily then levels off into a delightful grassy, woodland walk just inside the upper limit of trees. Emerging at a wall, there are open fields beyond leading to Byland Moor. Pass 2 forest rides L and re-enter woods, following the 3rd track L to reach Mount Snever Observatory tower. (If the way is lost hereabouts, most paths in the vicinity lead to the tower.)

The curious structure of blackened stone was erected in the first year of Queen Victoria's reign. 2 lines from an eroded inscription read,

> *'Happy the man who to these shades retires*
> *Who nature chains and whom the muse inspires.'*

The path to Oldstead drops steeply through Snever Wood from the south corner of the tower, a little obscurely at first. Slippery after wet weather, height is quickly lost and a forestry road reached, along which turn R. At a T-junction in 300m, turn L, passing through a gateway onto a farm road and turning L down it. Go L again at the next junction and L once more onto a road up into Oldstead village.

At the 'Black Swan' inn, fork L on the Byland Abbey road and in 300m, turn R to Oldstead Grange. Pass through the farmyard and gateway onto a track to the bottom of the next field and go through the gate, uphill to the buildings of Cams Head. Pass to the L of the house and aim for the top ruins of Byland Abbey ahead. Where the farm road turns L, go R, then continue ahead, L of the stream. Proceed along more field edges then over pasture to a gate and the yard of College Farm. Now on the road again, turn R to the magnificient ruins of Byland Abbey.

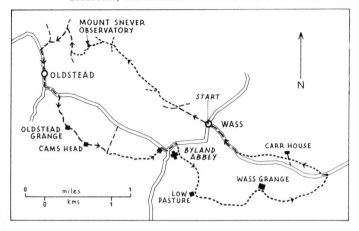

French Cistercian monks eventually founded Byland Abbey in 1177 after trying several sites in this area. One such, Old Byland (see Walk 16), was rejected by Abbot Roger on the grounds of competition from nearby Rievaulx Abbey's bells!

Byland's site was once a marsh and required systematic drainage - work which was to take 60 years to complete. Finally, the abbey had not only its own drinking water and sanitation, but fish and mill ponds and a market garden, making it entirely self-sufficient.

The remains we see today, extensive and elegant though they are, represent only a fraction of the original complex occupying the site until the Dissolution. Most imposing, perhaps, are the south transept and part of a wheel window 26ft (8m) in diameter in the west end. Apart from Byland Abbey's sheer size (larger than Rievaulx or Fountains), these ruins also contain detail of great interest, including well preserved decorative tiles. A closer look at the site is well rewarded and there is a small museum.

Walk along the Wass road *(the village is now only ½ mile away if a short-cut is required)* and take a field path R round the abbey's perimeter fence. Keep to the field edge as it veers L and leads down to a hollow, whereafter more fields are crossed to Low Pasture House Farm. Pass to the L, and beyond an old barn follow a boundary fence down to a small wooded knoll (Hessle Hill). Cross a stile and 2 fields to Wass Grange Farm, turning R before the farmyard and taking the field boundary track. *Ampleforth Abbey and College are visible to the east.*

Byland Abbey

Keep L of a fenced scrubby area used for rearing game birds and cross a stile into a field R. Climb across the field (no definite trod) and, keeping slightly R, follow a fence to the road at Jerry Carr Bank. Turn L and take a path off R, contouring along to cross Carr House access track at 2 gates, before walking downhill over a field towards the lower part of a belt of trees at a stream. A stile and the stream are crossed and 2 fields later the road rejoined, with Wass village now only a short distance to the R.

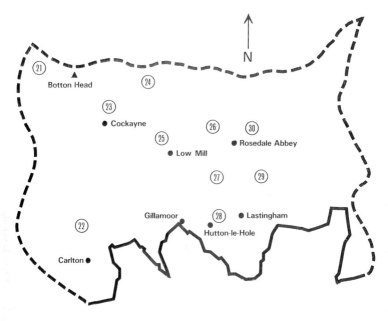

CHAPTER 3
THE SOUTHERN MOORS AND DALES

The northern limit to this chapter runs east, roughly along the main moorland watershed, but veers up to a point just short of the confluence of the Rivers Esk and Murk Esk. The western boundary is Bilsdale, the eastern boundary almost reaching Wheeldale and Newton Dale. In the south, the National Park perimeter zig-zags in and out from points along the A170 between Helmsley and Pickering.

The southern valleys - Riccal Dale, Bransdale, Kirk Dale, Farndale and Rosedale - penetrate deep into the moorland massif, the separating ridges correspondingly longer than their northern counterparts. There is some large-scale forestry in the west above Helmsley and in the east approaching Newtondale, but elsewhere plantations are mostly unobtrusive.

The pastoral, well-settled dales are steep sided and hemmed in by vast sweeps of heather moorland. Generously watered by their becks and sheltered from the worst weather, they are in many places extraordinarily beautiful, contrasting vividly with their harsh upland surroundings. A century ago, these dales witnessed a crescendo of activity as ironstone was extracted from rich seams in the dalesides, especially in Rosedale. A special railway was constructed over the very moortops to Ingleby Incline and its track bed now leads the walker past many relics of that era in our industrial history. Many of the tracks and paths over the moors were used by miners but date back much earlier in time: ancient tumuli and stones interrupt the broad horizons everywhere.

South of the moors proper lie the lower Tabular Hills, dissected by rivers draining south from the dales towards the Vale of Pickering. Almost all roads run roughly north-south, following the alignment of the land, but as in other regions of the Park, they are often narrow and twisting. They do, however, provide access right to the heart of this area, which the railway certainly cannot!

The Walks

Walk 21 follows the line of an ancient dyke along the edge of Urra Moor then takes a good track to Botton Head, highest point in the National Park; a well walked path leads back past numerous old boundary stones to the road at Hasty Bank. Forestry roads along Cowhouse Bank lead to Helmsley Moor and the line of the old Stokesley coach road, after which Walk 22 circles back through woodland and fields in the northern extremity of Riccal Dale.

Cockayne, at the head of Bransdale, is a remote spot indeed and the start of Walk 23 which passes the restored Bransdale Mill and heads up onto the old moortop Rudland Rigg coach road to reach Bloworth Crossing on the ironstone railway, returning through Bloworth Wood. Walk 24 circles the head of Farndale, using a stretch of the ironstone railway track bed, starting and finishing in the lonely dalehead itself.

West Gill is a branch of Farndale, explored by Walk 25 on its route to the top of Rudland Rigg and down to Church Houses in the dale, concluded by a riverside stroll through a Nature Reserve ablaze with daffodils in springtime. Walk 26 is a 'must' for students of industrial archaeology, following a branch of the Rosedale Ironstone Railway past the substantial remains of kilns, hoppers and mine workings on its way round Rosedale Head: a shorter variant keeps to the valley bottom. From more relics on Rosedale Bank Top, Walk 27 crosses rough heather moorland to visit the picturesque villages of Hutton-le-

Hole and Lastingham, returning past a fine stone cross. Hutton-le-Hole contains the Ryedale Folk Museum and Walk 28 is short enough to combine with viewing its many fascinating exhibits and installations.

From Lastingham, Walk 29 takes in Ana Cross and Rosedale Bank Top, thereafter flanking Spaunton Moor above the River Leven on lesser used paths back to the start. Rosedale Abbey attracts many visitors and is the base for Walk 30. Shorter than average, it climbs round to Northdale with superb views, before dropping to join the River Seven back to the village.

Wild Daffodils

WALK 21 CLAY BANK TOP - URRA MOOR DYKES - MEDD CRAG - BOTTON HEAD - CARR RIDGE - CLAY BANK TOP

6 miles (9.5km) - 3 hours - Moderate; exposed in bad weather

There are roadside pull-ins and a car park on the B1257 at Clay Bank Top, 2½ miles (4km) south-east of Great Broughton.

A forest track leads S from the car park and joins the main escarpment path *(used by numerous routes, including the Cleveland Way, Lyke Wake Walk, Coast to Coast, etc.)* which climbs L (E). Alternatively, walk S along the road and turn L onto it.

The way crosses a stile and increases in steepness, finally breaking

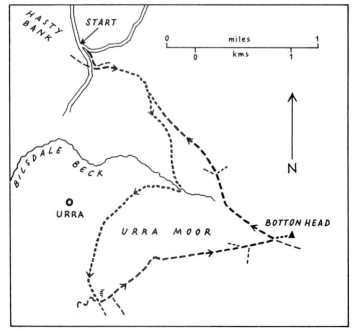

Hasty Bank (centre) and Carr Ridge (right) from Urra Moor Dykes

through a stony section in deeply eroded channels and reaching the top of Carr Ridge by a wall. *To the north are good views to Roseberry Topping, while behind (west) stands the impressive sweep of Hasty Bank.* Immediately beyond the wall, fork R off the main track, now following the clear line of prehistoric earthworks in the form of mound and ditch, contouring then gradually dipping along the W edge of Urra Moor.

These ancient dykes are a common feature of the North York Moors, sometimes a mile or more in length, but are hard to date with any certainty; some are thought to be medieval in origin. This particular example runs along the eastern crest of Bilsdale for about 3 miles (4.8km).

Continue S until the path and dyke cross a shallow ravine at the head of Bilsdale Beck *(above signs of old workings in the hillside)*, whereafter the direction swings W for a while before resuming a S course along the moor edge. *Glancing back, Carr Ridge and Hasty Bank form a dramatic 'V' in the escarpment profile, while down to the right are the farms of Upper Bilsdale.*

Reaching a wall above Urra, the path becomes very marshy by some springs. Either keep close to the wall or climb L a little above the wettest part: it improves after about 300m. Shortly after the wall swings down R by some conifer trees, Medd Crag appears up to the L, and a track coming up from Seave Green *(on the B1257 and a possible alternative starting point)* is joined as our route now turns L (NE) up onto the moor top.

In 200m, a broad, stony track comes in from the R and we continue ahead (NE then E) along it for approximately 1½ miles (2.4km) over the heathery expanses of Urra Moor. *Other hill features do no more from here than peep above its rim.*

The main Cleveland Way/Lyke Wake Walk etc. track is met at Round Hill on Botton Head: a narrow path leads E to the OS pillar on a tumulus - at 1489ft (454m) the highest point in the North York Moors National Park. *Views in clear weather (by no means a reliable condition in these parts!) are extensive rather than interesting.*

From the main track junction, walk back L (NW), dropping along the much used, stony track which is flanked by numerous boundary stones, a distinctive feature of this moor. In about a mile, the way levels off and rises slightly to meet a wall R, where this walk's outward leg forked off along the dyke. Simply drop down off Carr Ridge on the clear path, back to the road and car park.

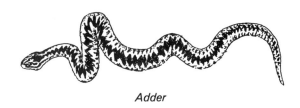

Adder

WALK 22 COW HOUSE BANK - ROPPA WOOD - HELMSLEY MOOR - SNAPER FARM - COWHOUSE BECK - HOWL WOOD FARM - RICCAL DALE WOOD - COW HOUSE BANK

9½ miles (15km) - 4½ hours - Moderate

From the large car park and picnic area provided by the Forestry Commission on Cow House Bank, north of Helmsley *(the quiet road continues over Pockley Moor and round the head of Bransdale)*, take a forest track NW along the level bank top. Ignore turnings off L and R, and after about a mile (1.6km), trees on the R give way to stunning views NE over Pockley Moor and Rudland Rigg and even as far as the northern escarpment.

Some 2 miles (3.2km) from the start, the track reaches a metalled lane from Helmsley at a large abstract sculpture by a bench. *The sculpture, by Austin Wright, was installed in 1977 to enhance the view and certainly the big hollow rims focus parts of the distant landscape in interesting ways; almost inevitably, its appearance resulted in considerable controversy.*

Ahead to the NW, atop Helmsley Bank, stands a triangulation pillar; the bridleway to it continues on round Rievaulx and Ayton Banks, down to the junction of Bilsdale with Ryedale just east of Hawnby. Here on the northern edge of the tabular hills, we are standing on corallian limestone, while the heather moors farther north are of sandstone.

Our route descends R down the lane, directly towards the TV Transmitting Station mast on Bilsdale West Moor. Where the tarmac ends at a junction of tracks, keep straight on at first, then fork L through Roppa Wood. Emerging from the trees, there are sudden views L (W) over to Easterside Hill and the moors to the NW.

From the plantation corner, a right-of-way is shown on maps going due N over heather moor, gradually rising along Carr Cote Ridge for a mile or so (1.5km) to the remains of a cross, near the highest point on Helmsley Moor. This path, once the old coach road to Stokesley, is visible from a distance but is less distinct on the ground. If the gentle climb up it is made, retrace steps to Roppa Wood corner to continue this route; in bad weather, give it a miss altogether.

We now follow a track R (NE), looping away from the plantation edge, then rejoining it when Potter House comes into view R. Walk

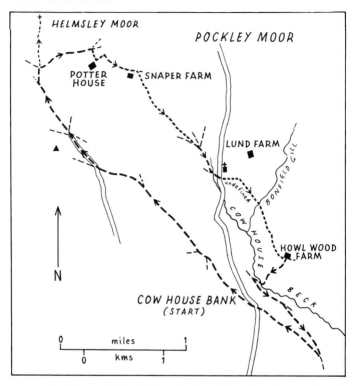

past the buildings (still a field away) alongside a wire fence, and at the 2nd wall, go through a gate and make a bee-line for the house. Just before the access gate, turn L down the field edge by a wall. Cross a brook L of 2 trees and climb a wall and ditch in the vicinity of a shed (a right-of-way but no stile). Turn R onto a brackeny track and head for the roofs of Snaper Farm, now derelict and used as barns. Pass to their L to reach a gate at the edge of East Moor Wood and turn R along the tree edge by a wire fence.

The way now swings R then L into a heathery forest track which gradually descends to meet a broad, rough forest road. Turn L to a junction of tracks on the forest edge and continue forward through a gate. Cowhouse Beck is crossed at a ford/footbridge, and a gate leads up into a lane. Fork L and arrive at the public road serving upper Riccal Dale.

Modern sculpture on Helmsley Bank

Directly opposite is a gate and public bridleway sign which indicates our way ahead over rough pasture. *The tiny chapel in a cluster of pine trees at Church Plantation is used by a community scattered widely over moors and forest in this locality.* Beyond a stand of trees, keep ahead but then bear R along a field fence to a gate at its narrowest far corner. Cross Bonfield Gill on a footbridge and climb up pathless, brackeny slopes (just E of S) to a wall. This leads round to a gate at Howl Wood Farm. Go through the farmyard and turn down R on the farm road for 2 field lengths to the ford/footbridge over Cowhouse Beck.

Here turn R (upstream) to a junction where a good forest track is taken sharp L (SE). In about 500m, fork R, climbing through pine forest and at the next junction doubling back sharp R (NW). This leads up to the public road, across which is the car park on Cow House Bank.

WALK 23 COCKAYNE - BRANSDALE MILL - SPOUT HOUSE - SHAW RIDGE - RUDLAND RIGG - BLOWORTH CROSSING - BLOWORTH WOOD - COCKAYNE

9 miles (14.5km) - 4 hours - Moderate; middle section exposed in bad weather

Bransdale, some 11 miles (18km) north of Helmsley, is as remote as anywhere in the North York Moors National Park. Although south facing, its back to the highest slopes around Botton Head, it is closer to the escarpment than to the Vale of Pickering: but that is as the crow flies, and the only way over those 3 miles (5km) is on foot.

Cockayne, where this walk begins, is a tiny settlement tucked into the northernmost corner of Bransdale. The Lodge belongs to Lord Feversham and the little chapel to the east dates from medieval times. There are broad, grassy verges beside the dale road below Bransdale Lodge, the only other feasible car parking being to the south at Spout House - an alternative start to the route.

From Cockayne, walk E along the road, down and up over Hodge Beck and round several bends to Cow Sike Farm. Turn R through the farmyard, go through a gate ahead and down a field to a ladder stile. Beyond, reedy pasture leads to another stile, whence stone steps drop to Bransdale Mill.

There has been a mill here since the 13th century, though the present

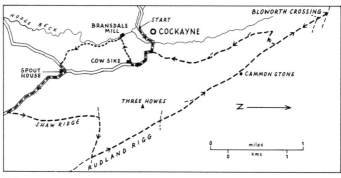

Bransdale Mill

buildings are mainly 19th century, the result of development by a William Strickland and embellished with classical inscriptions by his talented son Emmanuel, at one time vicar of Ingleby Greenhow. The elegant mill complex is now owned by the National Trust, is being carefully restored and is well worth taking time to look round.

The walk turns L from the bottom of the stone steps, along the E bank of Hodge Beck and through a gate into a field. Go down between 2 rowan trees and through a wall gap by a brook, after which climb L above a small hillock, pass through another gate and along a fence by trees. Drop to cross a wooded feeder stream, then go ½-L across a field, aiming at a wall corner just L of a large tree. Follow the wall to a gate and cross the next field in the same direction, passing through a gate and over a brook. Swing L through the next gate and up a track by a stream towards Spout House Farm ahead. A stile leads onto the public road, along which turn L, through the farm, turning sharp R at a junction and walking up past a telephone box.

Continue up the road (SE) for almost a mile (1.5km) until, at the top of a rise, turn back L on a track at a sign 'No Access for Motor Vehicles'. *(The right-of-way shown on some maps short-cutting this acute angle does not exist on the ground and the going is very rough.)* The track proceeds N along Shaw Ridge, becoming sandy and grassier and passing a conspicuous cairn-topped mound.

At a T-junction by grouse butts, turn R, crossing the shallow valley of Ouse Gill. At the next junction in about 600m, turn L onto the broad Rudland Rigg old road. *(A continuation ahead (E) leads easily down into Farndale near Church Houses.) We are now walking on the old coach road between Kirkbymoorside and Stokesley/Guisborough. It takes a remarkably straight, not to say audacious, line well above the 1000ft (305m) level for over 8 miles (13km) and is a splendid moortop walk for most of its length.*

A marker stone inscribed 'Kirby Rode' is passed; *lifting our sights to the E, the Lion Inn, Blakey Rigg and the course of the Rosedale Ironstone Railway can be seen. To the L are the Three Howes tumuli, visible from afar.* At a cairn, a grassy track leaves R (E) to upper Farndale, while the overgrown track L (W) would lead back down to the road near Cow Sike Farm should a short-cut be required.

Bloworth Wood is soon in view ahead L, and there are excellent views S down Bransdale. Beyond the Cammon Stone - a curiously shaped and marked monolith - the track starts to drop gently and a L turn-off sweeps down towards the end of Bloworth Wood. Providing weather and inclination are both favourable, however, an easy ½-mile (.8km) farther on along the moortop brings us to Bloworth Crossing.

The Rosedale Ironstone Railway plied between the Rosedale mines and Battersby, near Middlesborough, during the latter half of the 19th century and Bloworth Crossing was permanently manned. Today, it is still a notable intersection, especially to walkers on the Lyke Wake Walk, the Coast to Coast and other long distance routes. (For more details on the Rosedale ironstone industry, turn to Appendix 3 and Walks 24 and 26.)

Retrace steps to the turn-off sweeping down to Bloworth Wood. At the bottom, go through a gate and turn L along the forest road, gradually descending and reaching a gate where younger conifers R (at the time of writing) allow views of Bransdale Moor. Gates lead through a narrow belt of trees and out to the road. Turn R down and up over Hodge Beck, back to the unfenced verges below Bransdale Lodge.

WALK 24 WETHER HILL FARM - ESK HOUSE - FARNDALE HEAD - COURSE OF THE ROSEDALE IRONSTONE RAILWAY - BLOWORTH CROSSING - RUDLAND RIGG OLD ROAD - WETHER HILL FARM

7½ miles (12km) - 3 to 3½ hours - Moderate; exposed for most of the way in bad weather

Roads, though narrow and twisting, reach the isolated farms on both sides of Upper Farndale. Any car parking spot should be chosen with care so as not to block gateways or obstruct the passage of traffic, including tractors.

The route starts at a metal gate and 'Public Footpath' sign, one field's length above Wether Hill Farm. Go down (NE) through the farmyard and pass through a gate into fields, keeping downhill with fence and wall on the L. In the 2nd field, bear ½-R along by a wall,

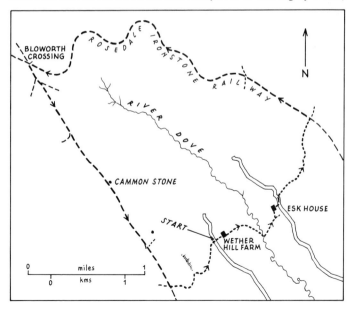

On the track bed of the Rosedale Ironstone Railway

continuing round the field edge. At the stream ahead (Gill Beck), cross a wall stile and walk R along the bank to a footbridge. A feeder stream is now followed uphill and a good track joined to Esk House (not to Lendersfield House as shown on some maps).

Turn L up the public road for about 75m, then take a bridleway off R, climbing delightfully over grassy and brackeny slopes with a stream first on the R, then on the L. Keep straight ahead, follow an old hollow way filled with reeds and pass to the L of a wooded dell. Cross a tumbledown wall ½-L and head on up towards isolated trees below the skyline. *The old railway course is easily identifiable if figures happen to be walking along it.* Still following the stream up, the path gradually improves and finally reaches the track bed at a sign 'Esk Valley Walk' pointing N over towards Esklets at the head of Westerdale.

The Rosedale Ironstone Railway was a truly remarkable undertaking, as anyone who walks its course will appreciate: it is one thing to travel on foot

The Cammon Stone and distant Bransdale

across these high moors, but quite another to run a railway over them. During the 1870's when the industry was at its height, trains carried iron-ore from the mines around Rosedale along this track, winding cleverly round the heads of Bransdale and Farndale without the need for bridge or tunnel. From 1370ft (418m) on Greenhow Moor, loaded wagons were lowered down the 1 in 5 Ingleby Incline by cable to Battersby, on their journey to the smelting mills of Tees-side and Durham.

Working conditions were often severe, both for the men who walked up from local village lodgings in all weathers to work in the mines, and for the railway crews who had to contend with gales, cold, and in bad winters, snowdrifts which would sometimes block the line for weeks. The track bed is now a familiar component in several long distance walks, including the Lyke Wake Walk and Coast to Coast. At Rosedale Head however, there are many more relics of the ironstone mining operations. For more details,

115

see Walk 26 and Appendix 3.

Turn L along the track bed, winding sinuously round Farndale. After 3 miles (5km), Bloworth Crossing is reached. *It was once permanently manned to safeguard the passage of man and beast across the railway, and a cottage stood nearby. It is as bleak a situation as one would care to imagine. The fact that permanent habitations were built and occupied the year round on these exposed moortops bears witness to the importance and vigour of the ironstone industry during its hey-day.*

Bloworth Crossing is a turning point for walkers on the Cleveland Way who have just traversed Urra Moor and now proceed north along the escarpment and down to Kildale. We also change direction, but to SE, along the old Stokesley/Guisborough to Kirkbymoorside coach road over Rudland Rigg. *For most of its way, it runs as straight as an arrow and well above the 1000ft (305m) contour.*

The broad, stony road passes above Bloworth Wood to the R. Ignore a R turn down to it, but about ½ way along watch out for the Cammon Stone on your L - an enigmatic monolith on a parish boundary at the top of a gentle rise. 1¼ miles (2km) later, a cairned grassy track leaves L (E) (opposite another, more vegetated track going W). This leads us down, increasingly steeply, to an overgrown, walled enclosure by Fox Hole Crag. Cross the stream here and follow the sunken way L then R, down past the enclosure. The path is not easy to see in summer due to bracken, but fortunately it keeps down by the stream, boggy in places, to meet a wall on the R. Pass through a gate by a telegraph pole and drop to the road at the starting point above Wether Hill Farm.

WALK 25 LOW MILL - WEST GILL -
RUDLAND RIGG - CHURCH HOUSES -
FARNDALE NATURE RESERVE -
LOW MILL

*6½ miles (10.5km) - 3 to 3½ hours - Moderate; middle
section more exposed in bad weather*

*The walk starts at Low Mill, about 7 miles (11km) north of Kirkbymoor-
side, by the River Dove in Farndale. (There are a small car park, public
toilets and a Post Office here.)*

Walk uphill (NW) towards the dale head, and in 500m turn L at a
sign 'Bridleway to Rudland Rigg', leading up the access track to Horn
End Farm. Keep straight on between the farm and Horn End
Cottages (up to the R), through a gate and onto a grassy bridleway. 2
more gates are passed going along above trees. Continue ahead past a
barn and through a very narrow field, over a stile, keeping to the L of
the wall at a bridleway sign. Flanking more trees, go through a gate
and turn L over West Gill Beck's footbridge.

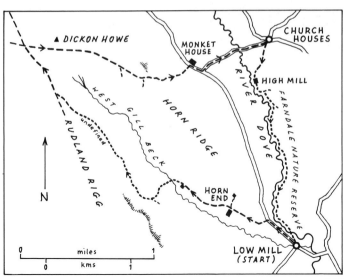

The valley of West Gill

We are now out onto rough pasture and need to keep L, parallel to a wall, before passing through another gate at a bridleway sign. At first, the track stays L, but soon swings R uphill. It is best to keep a little to the L through bracken until a shallow groove and a sign appear ahead where a vague track comes in from the L. Turn R along it, climbing to meet the wall above at a gate.

The following stretch, rising beneath Double Crag to the top of Rudland Rigg, is easier to follow in spring before bracken has obscured the path; with care, however, there should be no difficulty in keeping to the correct line.

Beyond the wall, keep up along the L bank of a reedy stream, in a short while crossing the equally marshy bed of a feeder stream L. Soon the main stream veers L, coming down from its source, and our route crosses it at a boggy area. There is now a clearer path through the bracken, generally NW and parallel to the crags above. It follows a shallow groove, then levels off somewhat, with marvellous views R (E) back down the verdant West Gill valley, an offshoot of Farndale, its patchwork of fields contrasting with the sweep of Horn Ridge above.

Despite more heavy bracken, the path persists, but when it reaches a hollow way in the vicinity of old tips and another stream bed, it is badly overgrown and the higher sides offer easier progress. Maintaining its NW direction, with West Gill to the R, the way leads towards the valley head, contouring along and gradually becoming more distinct and grassy. Eventually it passes some shooting butts L and emerges onto the Rudland Rigg old road.

This is a superb spot in anything but the worst weather; even in summer, you are unlikely to meet another human being for many a mile. Extensive views in all directions and a strong sense of unrestricted open space epitomise these high tops, so that enduring impressions are of cloud shadows over purple heather above red roofs and field patterns in the dales below. It is a landscape peopled only by sheep.

Turn R on the broad, stony road and at the next crossroad turn R on a good hard track E across a vast expanse of heather above the head of West Gill. *Dickon Howe, 100m to the L, is topped by a curious pile of stones, and soon views open out ahead over upper Farndale.* The track begins to descend, badly subsided in places, finally reaching the public road opposite derelict Monket House. Turn R, then L down to Church Houses hamlet.

At the Feversham Arms pub, take the metalled lane R signed 'Farndale Nature Reserve'. Go through a gate at the sign 'Public Path to Low Mill' and walk round L by a hedge to High Mill Cottage. *All that remains of its original water-wheel is a massive wooden axle, and the buildings are uninhabited at the time of writing.*

Our route now follows a well-walked path, muddy after wet weather, which threads its way picturesquely over stiles and round shady field corners by the River Dove. *Farndale is famous above all for its daffodils. At one time, the flowers were collected indiscriminately by visitors, particularly after the advent of motor transport earlier this century. Some people even used scythes, and there was some commercial exploitation of the blooms, in addition to damage by trampling. In 1955, a local nature reserve was set up, making the picking of daffodils illegal and ensuring their survival. In early spring, the 5 miles (8km) between Lowna and Church Houses are ablaze with the yellow flowers and receive many sightseers.*

119

Rudland Rigg

A footbridge crosses the Dove just below Low Mill and leads quickly up to the car park in the village.

WALK 26 THORGILL - HILL COTTAGES - EAST MINES - COURSE OF THE IRON-STONE RAILWAY ROUND ROSEDALE HEAD - BLAKEY JUNCTION - SHERIFF'S PIT - THORGILL

8½ miles (14km) - 3 to 4 hours - Moderate; exposed in bad weather

Thorgill lies about 1½ miles (2.5km) north-west of Rosedale Abbey along Daleside Road. It has limited car parking space and care must be taken not to obstruct private access. The hamlet was originally based on a small cluster of farmsteads, later around one shop, a chapel and a mill.

Named after the Norse war-god, Thorgill once housed men working Sheriff's Pit ironstone mine just up to the west. It was one of the most important mines in Rosedale, a valley which witnessed intense industrial activity for some 50 years, from the 1870's onwards: beds, it was said, were never cold, as shift replaced shift. Although the landscape is green and pleasant again, the scars are still there. No longer the eyesores they once were, the thinly overgrown railway tracks, workings, spoil heaps, kilns and

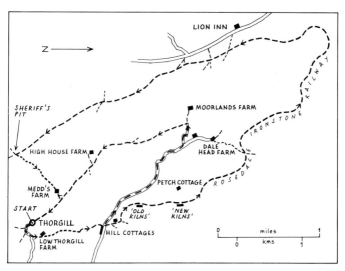

hoppers vividly recall a fascinating chapter in Rosedale's history.

More than any other, this walk takes us a century back in time and passes many sites of interest concerning the local ironstone industry.

NOTE: Although the track bed of the old ironstone railway is walked by many people, it is not a definitive right-of-way.

Start the route by walking towards Rosedale Abbey and turning L (at a R bend) on a lane down to Low Thorgill Farm. Go through the gate ahead-L marked 'Public Footpath' and walk ½-L down the field to a footbridge over Gill Beck. The way ahead up the next field is an old paved causeway, typical of many in this area of Yorkshire. Go over another footbridge and up the following field to a gap in a hedge, whence our now rutted track veers L and emerges at a kissing gate by some lock-up garages. Keep L up the lane to join the public road at Hill Cottages. Cross the road and climb the lane, past a building (the old 'Depot Cottage') and go through a metal gate onto an earthy track.

We have reached the site of 'The Depots' - Rosedale Goods Station at High Baring and the south-eastern terminus of the ironstone railway whose course runs for 7½ miles (12km) round Rosedale Head. A long row of cottages once stood here, in addition to a goods shed, stone coal cells and the 'Depot Cottage'. The station was closed in 1928.

Keep L beyond the ruined goods shed and walk along the old cinder track bed (not to the R of a large bank). Soon an impressive row of masonry arches appears on the R - ruins of the 'Old Kilns' which are still moderately intact. *These kilns were used to 'roast off' carbonic acid gas and water from the iron-ore, reducing its transported weight. The ore was not cooled before being moved from the kilns, so metal-bodied wagons were employed.*

500m further on stands more derelict masonry at East Mines, directly above Petch Cottage at an area known as High Baring. *These are the 'New Kilns', situated near the still visible multi-level sidings which serviced the mines. Substantial tips of calcine waste from the kilns accumulated on the slopes below them; when its commercial value was realised, before the mines finally closed down, the waste was removed for processing in Middlesborough between 1920 and 1927.*

Whilst proceeding ahead, it is easy to look around at the views; a glance back reveals the stump of East Mines ventilating shaft chimney. A couple of arms of Gill Beck are crossed and the track passes the remains of Black Houses, once linesmen's cottages but now just a shell and chimney. The track bed continues on round its terrace in the daleside, past a bridleway descent L (SW) to Dale Head Farm *(a possible short-cut back to Thorgill)*, and round the sharp corner of Nab Scar.

The remains of Black Houses, East Rosedale

Thereafter, it swings round the dale head, crossing the headwaters of Reeking Gill and the River Seven on embankments and assuming a S direction.

Running parallel to the road along Blakey Ridge, the track bed comes within 250m of the Lion Inn, a lonely public house once patronised by miners from the many coal and ironstone workings in the vicinity, and now a popular refreshment stop for motorists and walkers - at 1325ft (403m) above sea level.

A little way to the south, at 1200ft (366m) above sea level, stood a small community of 7 railwaymen's cottages called Little Blakey, and from the nearby junction, the railway line began a moortop course north-west, looping round the head of Farndale before reaching Ingleby Incline Top. Wagons filled with iron-ore were lowered here by cable to join the main rail network at the foot of the escarpment.

Continue following the track bed, E of S down Blakey Ridge for a further 2½ miles (4km). At Sledge Shoe Bents, site of a former reservoir supplying the locomotives, ignore a path off L down to High House Farm. Soon after the daleside gradient levels off, a path junction is reached near Sheriff's Pit (L) - *both a good viewpoint over*

Rosedale and one of the major ironstone mines. The pit-head winding gear ruins and a fenced off shaft are still clear to see.

From here, it is a short descent to Thorgill. Take the 1st path L (NE), which keeps to the R of a small stream valley. The slope steepens and we veer R above a rocky outcrop. Once through the intake wall, carry on downhill in the same NE direction, with a wall to your L, to arrive at Medd's Farm *(riding school, camping)*. Turn R past the buildings and R again on a rough road which joins the public road to enter Thorgill hamlet.

NOTE: A shorter version of the above walk, keeping to the dale bottom, follows the route as far as Hill Cottages. Here turn L along Daleside Road (actually a cul-de-sac) and in 2 miles (3km), turn L down a steep lane just before Red House Farm. Cross the infant River Seven at a ford, pass through a gate and walk up the lane towards Moorlands Farm. About ½ way up, turn L over rough grazing and go through a gate onto the old Daleside Road, a well-defined field track which threads its way pleasantly back down the dale. *There are good views NE of the East Mines complex along the valley flanks.* After High House Farm, the track improves greatly and leads past little static caravans and horses below Medd's Farm *(it's a riding school and has a camp site)*, thence down into Thorgill. Total distance 4½ miles (7km) - about 2½ hours.

WALK 27   ROSEDALE BANK TOP -
HUTTON RIDGE - HUTTON-LE-HOLE -
LASTINGHAM - ANA CROSS -
ROSEDALE BANK TOP

*8 miles (13km) - 3½ to 4 hours - Moderate; partly
exposed in bad weather.*

*There is ample car parking space at Rosedale Bank Top, as well as several
interesting relics of the ironstone industry. (For fuller details, please see
Walk 29.) This is also a very fine viewpoint over Rosedale and is only ¾
mile (1200m) from the village of Rosedale Abbey, though the gradient up
Rosedale Bank is 1 in 3!*

The walk starts SW along the moor road towards Hutton-le-Hole.
After about ½ mile (1km), beyond some grouse butts and a slight L
bend in the road, look out for 2 parallel tracks branching off R. Take
the 2nd of these, grassy at first, but soon giving out, and continue on
down in the same direction over rough heather towards a good track
visible ahead.

The way drops boggily over Loskey Beck to a sheepfold, thereafter
joining the plain track coming in from the L. Turn R along it (still
SW), following a line of shooting butts and descending slightly to ford
another arm of Loskey Beck. Climbing gently, a waymarking post is

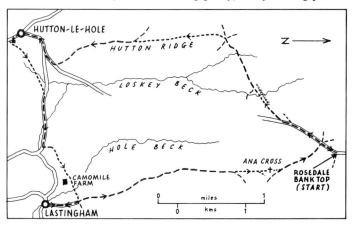

Old ironstone kilns at Rosedale Bank Top

soon reached at an intersection. Walkers are directed off L between 2 shooting butts on a clear path dropping pleasantly S down Hutton Ridge, with lovely views ahead. *Sheep use the path too, increasing its breadth lower down.*

Eventually we meet Lodge Road, a wide, stony track on the ridge between Loskey and Hutton becks, and turn L along it. It becomes metalled and drops to the public road just above Hutton-le-Hole. *(If time is short, excluding a visit to Hutton-le-Hole, cross this road and proceed down over grass for about 200m to the next road, turning L along it. In 400m, the main route comes in from the R.)*

To visit Hutton-le-Hole, turn R down the public road and follow it round L (S) past a car park into the village. *(For full details of this charming and interesting place, please turn to the next walk 28.)* Instead of retracing steps out of the village, take a path behind the chapel, just S of the Ryedale Folk Museum, keep L of the bowling green and cross a series of fields on a path in a NE direction. A footbridge crosses Fairy Call Beck, whereafter the public road is met and taken R towards Lastingham.

Just before the road bridge crosses Loskey Beck, turn L on a grassy track, with allotments and beautifully maintained hawthorn hedges R. Pass through a gate and follow the good track which narrows to a path to skirt outside an intake wall and fence. Pass Camomile Farm, keeping L of the fence, and continue along the brackeny path with trees and wall to the R.

Our route now drops steeply to a hollow, crosses Hole Beck and climbs by a wall. At the moor gate near a seat, turn down R into a lane, past a hotel and into Lastingham, a picturesque village with old houses, Post Office, a few shops and refreshment places.

To return to Rosedale Bank Top, follow the 1st part of Walk 29 from Lastingham, past Ana Cross, back to the start of this walk.

Lambing Time

WALK 28 HUTTON-LE-HOLE - LINGMOOR WOOD - SPAUNTON - HUTTON-LE-HOLE

4 miles (6.5km) - 2 hours - Easy

Signs of early Neolithic farmers and herdsmen, such as their arrowheads and pottery, pre-date recorded history, as do those of the Roman era and the Saxons. However, Hutton-le-Hole does appear in the great Domesday survey of 1085/86 as Hoton, thereafter undergoing several name changes, from Hege-Hoton, Hoton under Heg and Hewton, to Hutton-in-the-Hole by the 17th century; the present form appears only in the 19th century.

The village lies in a hollow between two limestone headlands of the Tabular Hills (so-called from their flat-topped, table-like appearance) which slope gently south and form a marked contrast to the bleak moors

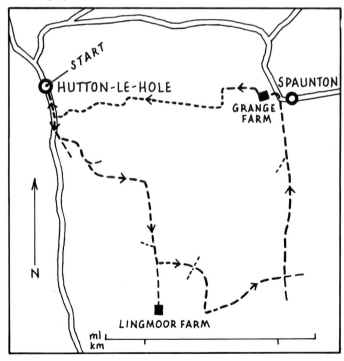

The Ryedale Folk Museum, Hutton-le-Hole

farther north.

There has been a strong tradition of crafts here for centuries, including spinning and weaving, tanning and milling. Lime-burning, coal mining and the ironstone industry also left their marks and in past ages, the village would have seemed a very different, vastly more earthy place than the quiet and well manicured spot admired by sightseers and visitors today.

An excellent booklet published by the North York Moors National Park Information Service and called 'The History of Hutton-le-Hole' will act as a guide, pointing out the many features of interest in the village. The Ryedale Folk Museum, however, is likely to draw most attention initially and is well worth an hour or two's browse. Opened in 1964, it contains the private collection of the Crosland family, housed in buildings and land bequeathed for the purpose. Assembled by Mr. B. Frank, curator from 1964 to 1979, the material is continually being added to. Exhibits are almost all local, reflecting daily life in Ryedale through many centuries. There are reconstructed interiors and whole buildings, shops, country crafts, farm machinery, a stable, foundries, glass furnace, barns and many archaeo-logical remains.

This walk is a short one, assuming time has been spent in Hutton-le-Hole and the museum, and acting as a kind of 'digestif' for all the information and impressions absorbed. There is a car park to the north of the village, also a few shops, café and pub.

129

Cruck Cottage, Ryedale Folk Museum, Hutton-le-Hole

Opposite the last house at the S end of the village, fork L up a stony track and in 50m fork L again on a Public Bridleway. This veers R, through a gate and uphill, before levelling off and swinging L into a very pleasant green lane between fields. Turn R down Bottomfields Lane (still a field track) and when Lingmoor Farm is in view ahead, turn L down a rough bridleway between hedges. This climbs R into the edge of Lingmoor Wood.

Go through a gate out onto pasture and turn L alongside trees, with barns to the R. Another gate leads onto a good track (Lingmoor Lane) and at a junction, we turn L up Spauntons Lane. *At the time of the Domesday survey, almost the whole area around Hutton now under cultivation was already so used or down to pasture.*

The track becomes metalled and meets the public road just W of Spaunton (*a richer source of archaeological evidence of early settlement than any other local village, and a much larger place in medieval times than it is today*). Turn L and immediately L again, over a cattle grid, keeping R of a barn through Grange Farm. Turn R down a stony track as the waymarked route now follows field boundaries back towards Hutton. *There are continuing wide views over the Vale of Pickering and the Tabular Hills to the south.*

At the end of a long rising stretch, there is a sudden viewpoint R at a corner overlooking Spaunton Moor and Hutton Ridge and, farther away to the north-west, the TV transmitting mast on Bilsdale Moor. Follow signs R down a wall gap; the path drops past a ruined barn and beneath a canopy of trees and bushes. Cross a stile and another immediately R, now dropping more steeply down a bank to a small brackeny gully. Here turn R, then keep L on a path churned up by cattle, dropping to Fairy Call Beck. It is better to stay L where the ground is drier. Go over a stile and out to the road at the village's south end.

WALK 29 LASTINGHAM - ANA CROSS - ROSEDALE BANK TOP - RIVER SEVEN VALLEY - TRANMIRE BECK - LASTINGHAM

8 miles (13km) - 3½ to 4 hours - Moderate: partly exposed in bad weather

Lastingham lies in a pretty hollow on the broad ridge between Rosedale and Farndale. An attractive village with old houses ranged along its two streets, the most interesting feature are the remains of an 11th century Benedictine abbey, built on Celtic foundations and destroyed by the Danes in 862. The parish church now occupies the site, but the original Norman crypt is extremely well preserved. Local stories tell of its use for cock-fighting in the 18th century.

From the village centre, walk N up a cul-de-sac, past a hotel R, through a gate and out onto open moorland. Go slightly L of a hollow and take to the grassy track up Lastingham Ridge. The track soon becomes sandy between broad sweeps of heather and is accompanied by numerous cairns. Where it curves gently R, fork L by 2 cairns on a narrower path towards Ana Cross, now clearly visible ahead. In a few hundred metres, fork L again on an even narrower path through

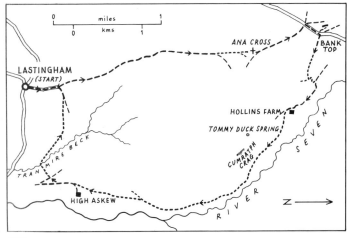

heather, but still cairned and soon becoming plainer.

Ana Cross is one of 50 or so such structures on the North York Moors, many now just socket stones with broken shafts. This example is, however, robust and intact, named after some long-forgotten person whose story could no doubt have been told many centuries ago. On the north-west horizon are the conspicuous Three Howes tumuli, and distant traffic can be made out on the moor road.

Leave Ana Cross and joint a good wide track leading W of N to the road at Rosedale Bank Top. *It was here that the Rosedale Ironstone Railway was opened officially on March 27th 1861. This southern terminus at 975ft (297m) above sea level, sustained a small community of railway employees, one of their cottages being subsequently used as a Youth Hostel from 1933 to 1950. All but one or two of the cottages have been demolished.*

Also at Bank Top was installed a row of kilns into which ore from the Hollins Mines to the south-east was tipped and roasted to drive off water and carbonic acid gas - a process called calcination which reduced the ironstone's weight for transportation. The crumbling masonry of the kilns still stands, though the shutters and ironwork have long since gone.

Until 1972 when it was demolished, the chimney of the engine-house which powered the Hollins Mines incline tramway winding gear was a famous landmark. Water for the steam boilers (and for railway loco-motives) came from a reservoir just to the west, still in evidence; it was fed from Jewel Mere by leat. The road up to Bank Top from Rosedale Abbey was constructed by the ironstone company and, at a gradient of 1 in 3, is one of the steepest in Britain.

Turn R along the road at signs 'Maximum gradient 1:3' and 'Unsuitable for lorries and caravans'. On a L bend where the road begins its descent of Rosedale Bank, take a path off R alongside a gully and follow the track bed of the old incline tramway down brackeny hillside (SE). At a small copse, continue alongside a wire fence and through a gap in the fence ahead. Drop through more bracken, still on the old tramway, along by a fence in a groove through old mine spoil heaps. *Up to the R were some of the most productive ironstone workings in Rosedale, now mostly overgrown.*

Where a small marshy valley fed by springs opens up R, go through a gate L (underneath barbed wire, but on a right-of-way), then walk ½-R down a vague track, twisting R over pasture. Keep well R of buildings below and join a rough track down to a gate, turning R along the unsurfaced farm road. Pass through a gate and fork R before Hollins Farm, up a grassy track between old gateposts. By a wall corner at the top, fork L alongside a wall (not ahead up the clear track

Ana Cross

through bracken).

Our path now contours delightfully along bracken-clad hillside, with pastoral views L over the River Seven. There is a boggy stretch below Tommy Duck Spring, then up to the R appears Cumratph Crag (pronunciation uncertain!). The path becomes rockier and descends gently, the valley opposite ever more wooded as the western edge of Cropton Forest is approached.

Steep moorside to the R starts to level off and the way climbs gradually to the top of a long slope. Here fork L on the thinner of 2 paths over heather and bracken, cross a small stream and keep ahead outside the wall of a sparse plantation. The route runs prettily between wall and stream, but keep R of a marshy depression above High Askew Farm and continue alongside the wire boundary fence, finally turning R up a stony farm road.

At the top of the rise where a hedged wooden fence comes up on the

L, fork R on an indistinct old bridleway through low bracken. Veering R, it crosses a much clearer grassy track and there are good views ahead now over the open expanses of Spaunton Moor.

Maintaining the same general direction (SW), we drop into the bare valley of Tranmire Beck, keeping L by small trees and dropping to cross the beck on stepping stones. *(If in spate, it may be necessary to go back some 250m to the grassy track. Here, either walk N for about 800m and turn L on a path which crosses the valley higher up at the confluence of Grain Beck and Tranmire Beck; or walk S, rejoining the stony track from High Askew which leads to the public road (Ings Lane) a mile E of Lastingham.)*

Climb out of Tranmire Beck valley and follow a wire fence along R (NW), then a wall. When it veers L, aim for a stand of large trees ahead, passing them to join a deeply worn bridleway back to the moor gate, turning L down the cul-de-sac into Lastingham village.

Kestrel

WALK 30 ROSEDALE ABBEY - HARTOFT RIGG - NORTHDALE RIGG - NORTHDALE - ROSEDALE ABBEY

5 miles (8km) - 2½ to 3 hours - Moderate

This walk is centred on the picturesque village of Rosedale Abbey. Situated at the confluence of the River Seven and Northdale Beck, there is in fact no abbey here, just a fragment or two of a 12th century priory near the parish church. It was erected by William of Rosedale and its complement of Cistercian nuns remained there until the Dissolution of the Monasteries.

Rosedale itself is a charming, pastoral valley, though a century ago would have presented a very different face. The ironstone industry trans-

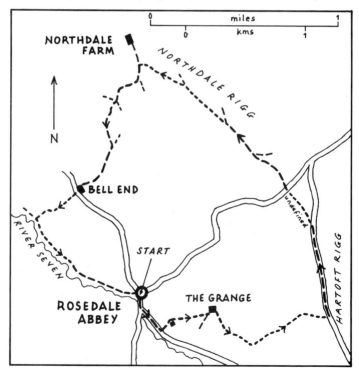

*formed the dalesides with its bustling activity, its buildings, railway lines,
mine workings and the concommitant pollution. Nature is a great healer.*
  *The Rosedale Circuit - an arduous 37 mile (59.5km) challenge walk
- starts and finishes at Rosedale Abbey. (See Chapter 5)*

From the village centre, take the Pickering road, pass the Coach
House Restaurant, and in about 200m turn L up the drive to a modern
farmhouse. Pass it on the L, go through a metal gate, then ½-R across
a field. 2 gates later, we turn L onto The Grange's farm drive. Go into
the yard of the lovely old farmstead and through a metal gate R.
Follow yellow arrows on a rough track with a wall R, through 3 fields
and climb a ladder stile. Now turn L uphill, with wall and fence to the
L, cross a double stile and head up to the R of the nearest plantation.
Walk steeply uphill to its edge, cross the stile and keep forward
through bracken and reeds, the way less distinct here. *(There are,
however, very fine views back over Rosedale.)* Cross another stile and
bear ½-R up a good path to the Hancow Road.
  Turn L along the tarmac, pass a path off L, and reach the end of
Russell's Wood plantation on the R. A 'Public Bridleway' sign here
incorrectly points NW across trackless heather and can be ignored.
Just before the road bends gently R, fork off L (NW) over heather
moor for about 500m (short-cutting the road junction corner), to meet
a correct bridleway sign, confirming our line.
  Cross the road *(a possible short-cut down to Rosedale Abbey, only 1¼
miles away)* and continue ahead on a very clear moorland track, soon
joined from the R by another from Brown Hill. Gently descending the
W slopes of Northdale Rigg, the track forks: we take the indistinct L
arm to a gate in a wall, thereafter keeping in the same direction (NW)
downhill. At a small marker stone, fork L on another rather vague
track which soon becomes clear, dropping through 2 gates to barns
and the lane from Northdale Farm. *Northdale is one of the remoter spots
in the North York Moors, infrequently visited and quite inaccessible in
winter conditions.*
  Turn L down the surfaced lane, round Bell Top hill's S flanks to
Bell End Farm and the public road. Turn L, then R on a signed
footpath immediately opposite the farm buildings. The way now
descends 2 fields with a hedge L, passes through a gate and along a
narrow path with a thin strip of trees R. Drop to the stream and
continue down its L bank, over a stile and up a muddy slope.
  Crossing another stile, the caravan/camping site becomes visible
below, alongside the River Seven just to the NW of Rosedale Abbey.
A stile and kissing gate lead onto the site itself, which is walked

through, past a playground, to turn L at a footpath sign. Rosedale Abbey village is now a stone's throw away.

Swaledale Ram

CHAPTER 4

THE EASTERN MOORS,
DALES AND COAST

Whitby and the last few miles of the River Esk's journey to the North Sea lie outside the National Park boundary, which forms this chapter's northern edge. The western limit extends just beyond the snaking course of Newton Dale to include Wheeldale. To the south, the National Park perimeter juts down to embrace Thornton Dale before swinging round north to the coast, excluding Scarborough.

The eastern moors, though lower than those farther west, are no less impressive and are even more subject to weather coming in off the North Sea: that dense, saturating sea fog known locally as a 'roak' is but one example. Boundless expanses of heather and ling are found here just as elsewhere in the Park, but the Forestry Commission has brought about a radical transformation by establishing extensive tracts of conifer forest, especially in the southern half of this area. The Visitor Centre at Low Dalby provides an insight into forestry life, and the Forestry Commission itself has set up numerous walking trails, picnic and parking areas and forest drives.

Dales in this area lack the organised alignment of those in the central moorlands and are more individual in character. There are several waterfalls ('fosses') around Goathland, as well as a magnificently preserved length of Roman Road and an Historical Railway Trail. In the south are many features of interest, including the Hole of Horcum, Fylingdales Early Warning Station and the Forge Valley Nature Reserve.

Another fine stretch of Heritage Coast leads down past Robin Hood's Bay, a most attractive fishing village under high cliffs at the end of a bay sweeping round to the rock formations at Ravenscar. Farther south still, the tiny cove of Hayburn Wyke is backed by a woodland Nature Reserve. Geology and wild-life join these attractions, while the dismantled Whitby to Scarborough railway provides scope for circular walks.

Reflecting the varied terrain in this eastern section of the National Park, walking ranges from easy strolls to more strenuous excursions, though (with one or two exceptions) the routes are not sustained high-level ones. During the summer season, the North York Moors

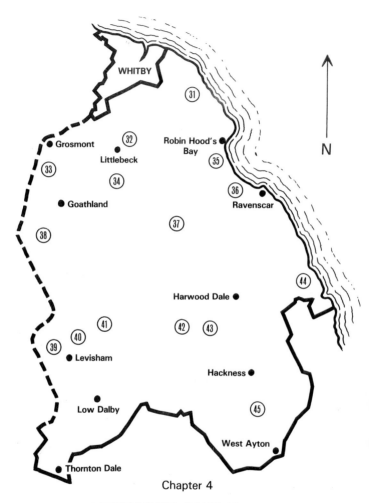

WHITBY

③①

● Grosmont ③② Robin Hood's ●
Bay
Littlebeck ③⑤
③③
③④ ③⑥
● Goathland Ravenscar ●
③⑦
③⑧

N

Harwood Dale ●

④① ④② ④③
④⓪
③⑨ ● Levisham

Hackness ●

● Low Dalby ④⑤

West Ayton ●

● Thornton Dale

Chapter 4

EASTERN MOORS, DALES AND COAST

④④

Railway Trust operates a steam service to stations along Newton Dale from Pickering to Grosmont - not only a romantic and nostalgic train ride in its own right, but also a very good way of finishing a day's walk or reaching a starting point. Main roads are the south-to-north A169 Pickering to Whitby and the A171 Whitby to Scarborough; the A170 runs west to east from Pickering to Scarborough. As in the rest of the Park, minor roads are tortuous and do not penetrate the central block of moors at all.

The Walks

Walk 31 acknowledges the town of Whitby (just outside the Park) by starting and finishing at its clifftop Abbey ruins. A good coast path (waymarked for the Cleveland Way which runs the length of the Heritage Coast from Saltburn to Filey Brigg) leads to Robin Hood's Bay, the return being along the track bed of the dismantled Whitby to Scarborough railway. Walk 32 is a short and easy woodland descent from Falling Foss to Littlebeck and back along the valley side. Few people will fail to be interested by Walk 33 which is based round the Historical Railway Trail from Goathland to Grosmont along George Stephenson's original line: Grosmont is the northern terminus of the North York Moors Railway.

Walk 34 circles the head waters of May Beck from Falling Foss and takes in the Whinstone Ridge, York Cross and pleasant forest paths. Walks 35 and 36 explore the villages of Robin Hood's Bay and Ravenscar, and the geologically fascinating coast between them, using the dismantled coast railway to return to their respective starts.

Walk 37 is a true moorland hike from Jugger Howe Beck, along the Lyke Wake Walk path to the oldest of the North York Moors crosses on Lilla Howe: a good track leads down to the coffee shop start. Another moortop excursion, Walk 38 climbs from Goathland to Two Howes Rigg and Simon Howe, along a stretch of the Lyke Wake Walk, through forest and out to the Roman Road on Wheeldale Moor. Thereafter, it descends West Beck gorge to Mallyan Spout waterfall and Goathland.

The North York Moors Railway runs along Newton Dale close to Levisham, and Walk 39 gives good views of trains, as well as the opportunity to catch one in either direction from Levisham station. Walk 40 provides an experience of the great natural hollow, the Hole of Horcum, both from above and down inside its enclosing hillsides. Walk 41, starting from picturesque Levisham, does the same but

141

Hackness Hall, Walk 45.

continues on to Malo Cross by Fylingdales Early Warning Station 'golf balls', past Blakey Topping to the extraordinary Bridestones Nature Reserve. Woodland and riverside paths down Stain Dale lead back via Lockton village.

Walks 42 and 43 have a forestry flavour about them. Walk 42 climbs to Langdale Rigg viewpoint, circling back on part of the waymarked Reasty to Allerston Forest Trail. Walk 43 from Reasty Bank descends lovely Whisper Dales then swings north through Broxa Forest on a delightful path alongside the River Derwent. A stiff climb leads to the bank top and a forestry road with wide views back to the start.

Right in the National Park's south-east corner on Walk 44, Hayburn Wyke is an idyllic cove and waterfall, backed by a woodland Nature Reserve rich in wild flowers. A section of clifftop walking is followed by a return on the dismantled coast railway. Walk 45 from West Ayton crosses pleasant hilly farmland to Hackness Hall, stately home of Lord Derwent, then follows the River Derwent back, first in open country then through the beautiful confines of Forge Valley, a deeply wooded Nature Reserve.

142

WALK 31 WHITBY ABBEY - SALTWICK BAY - HAWSKER BOTTOMS - NESS POINT - ROBIN HOOD'S BAY - DISMANTLED RAILWAY - WHITBY ABBEY

12½ miles (20km) - 5 to 6 hours - Moderate: cliff path exposed in places

Whitby, although outside the National Park boundary, is a fascinating town and harbour and should not be missed by any visitor to the area, walker or otherwise. A detailed description of its many attactions lies outside the scope of this guide, but there are several publications available from bookshops and information centres which deal with its history and associations.

Whitby Abbey, where this walk begins, was founded in AD657 by St.

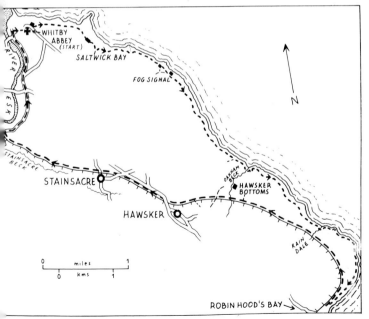

Hilda, daughter of the King of Northumberland. Occupied by both nuns and monks, the abbey was attacked by Viking invaders on several occasions and was finally abandoned following the Dissolution of the Monasteries in 1539. Unfortunately, it was further damaged by German warships aiming their fire at the nearby Coastguard Station during World War I.

Some walkers will have reached the Abbey by climbing the famous 199 steps from the Old Town to the Church of St. Mary (although a road approach is also possible). Views back across Whitby harbour, with its clusters of red-roofed houses and narrow streets, have hardly changed since Captain Cook's day, except for the modern craft which have replaced the sailing ships so evocatively recorded in some of Frank Meadow Sutcliffe's photographs a century later.

A roadside gate at Abbey Farm leads onto the coast path, used by holidaymakers from Saltwick Bay holiday camp as well as Cleveland Way walkers (for whom the route is well signed). From the Coastguard lookout, the path is close to the cliff edge, only turning inland at the holiday camp.

Cross a metalled lane and continue on the waymarked coast path S of Saltwick Bay to the lookout and Fog Signal *(hopefully not in operation as you pass!)*. Follow Cleveland Way signs carefully here to avoid going astray: the path proceeds along a level stretch beyond the Fog Signal, thereafter climbing to a signpost and stile on the edge of Beacon Hill.

From here onwards to Robin Hood's Bay, the path is easy to follow, though in places it hugs the precipitous cliffs rather too closely for comfort in windy weather. Two small valleys - Oak Beck below Hawsker Bottoms (campsite), and Rain Dale - provide steeper gradients and muddier going (in wet conditions), but otherwise the path is undulating and punctuated only by stiles.

Cliffs on this part of the Yorkshire coast are of boulder clay, highly susceptible to marine erosion. Ness Point is rounded and Robin Hood's Bay appears ahead, tucked down into the top of the bay which curves round to a conspicuous headland at Ravenscar.

Before dropping into the town itself (see Walk 35), double back NE off the coast path onto the track bed of the disused Whitby to Scarborough railway, now a 'Permitted Path' for walkers, cyclists and horse riders. This forms the basis for an easy 5 mile (8km) stroll back to the outskirts of Whitby. *On the way there are good sea views to begin with, changing to rural scenery as we pass the villages of High Hawsker and Stainsacre and descend gently above Cock Mill Wood.*

The mouth of the River Esk lies ahead and about 250m past the end

St. Mary's church above Whitby harbour

of Cock Mill Wood we turn R down onto the minor road past Larpool Hall. In a little over a mile, we have dropped to sea level in Whitby Old Town and, if necessary, can complete the circuit by climbing back up to the Abbey.

WALK 32 FALLING FOSS CAR PARK - LITTLEBECK - LEAS HEAD FARM - FALLING FOSS CAR PARK

3½ miles (5.5km) - 2 hours - Easy to moderate

Like Walk 34, this route starts at the car park above Falling Foss. Walk down the track to this delightful waterfall - a 30ft (9m) high cascade in beautiful deciduous woodland. Midge Hall stands nearby, but our way now turns R on a path by Little Beck (a Forest Trail), climbing slightly to the boundary of Newton House Outdoor Activities Centre. We descend to pass a huge boulder - The Hermitage - hollowed out as a shelter and dated 1790, thereafter keeping ahead down the wooded valley. An area of old quarry spoil heaps leads on to the road at Littlebeck hamlet, a tiny, picturesque settlement in a deep fold of the hills.

Turn L, cross Little Beck at the ford and turn immediately L onto a Public Bridleway which crosses Wash Beck and passes through a gate into Little Beck Wood Nature Reserve, administered by the Yorkshire Naturalists' Trust. Climb steadily on a clear path (muddy in places), eventually leaving the lovely deciduous woods and continuing on a track with trees to the R.

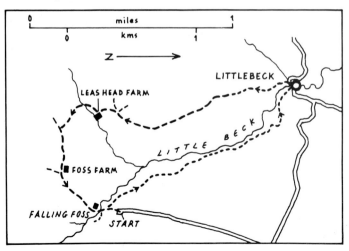

Falling Foss

Entering a green lane through a gate out of the Nature Reserve, with woods still on the R, we bear L at a Bridleway sign and walk up the edge of a large field on a grassy track. At the top, go through a gate and veer R a little to skirt Great Wood, with good retrospective views down Little Beck valley.

At the next gate, turn L onto a stony track down through Leas Head farmyard with its quaint duckpond, turning R (signed Falling Foss) through a gate and down over Parsley Beck. Here, bear L on a pleasant field track and at a T-junction and gate, turn L on another farm track past Foss Farm barns. This continues down, with woods R, to a bridge over May Beck near Midge Hall and Falling Foss, whereupon take the track back up to the car park.

Common Lizard

WALK 33 GOATHLAND - HISTORICAL RAILWAY TRACK - GROSMONT - CRAG CLIFF WOOD - GREEN END - ELLER BECK - GOATHLAND

6½ miles (10.5km) - 3½ hours - Moderate; possible return from Grosmont by train

Goathland's history stretches back beyond the 12th century. In 1267, the village and much of the surrounding land were given to the Earl of Lancaster by Henry III and, to this day, the Duchy of Lancaster still owns a good proportion of the common land.

With every justification, Goathland is a popular holiday and walking centre. The adjacent moors are particularly beautiful and full of interest, while in the immediate vicinity are found the North York Moors Railway, an Historical Railway Trail (which this walk includes) and several waterfalls - Mallyan Spout (see Walk 38), Water Ark Foss, Thomason Foss and Nelly Ayre Foss. ('Foss' sometimes appears as 'Force'.) Goathland is close to the Roman Road over Wheeldale Moor - one of the best preserved lengths in the country - and is only 9 miles (14.5km) from Whitby.

George Stephenson's original railway track from Whitby to Pickering was opened in 1836, but in those early days, carriages were scarcely more than stage-coaches mounted on bogies and were still horse-drawn. The 1 in 5 incline from Beck Hole was a persistent problem: wagons had to be hauled up to the 200ft (60m) contour by metal cable and there were a number of accidents, culminating in a fatality in 1865. That same year, a

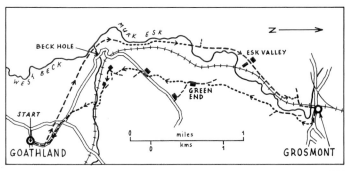

'Deviation Line' was finally blasted and Eller Beck bridged in 4 places - a massively expensive operation costing £50,000. But thereafter the line could take steam locomotives, as indeed it still does.

There is a car park near the village shops. Pass the public conveniences, turn L through a gate signed 'Grosmont' and walk down a wide, grassy track - the original route of the railway track. *Terraced cottages on the R were the homes of railway employees, and just past a large ash tree stands Ash Tree Cottage, once the waiting room at Bank Top.*

Cross the road and continue down the incline towards Beck Hole. *From 1836 to 1865, carriages were uncoupled and hauled from Beck Hole to Bank Top by cable.* The track crosses a road and becomes more stony before it reaches the bottom of the incline; a stream is eroding the path in places. *Incline Cottage is another Railway Company building and there is a fragment of iron rail as well as an old pump at the front.*

Keep straight on over Eller Beck on large stepping stones (actually the supports of a former bridge), which may be submerged in times of spate. If so, go back through Beck Hole village, L over the road bridge, and L past the first house, along by the beck. Turn R onto the track.

Over Eller Beck, there is a brass plaque on the site of Beck Hole Station bearing information about its use and closure. Follow the track R down through the delightful Blue Ber Wood (well waymarked), a detour made necessary by the destruction of the railway bridge in the 1930 floods.

Over the stile out of Blue Ber Wood, views open ahead of the Murk Esk valley and of the broad track bed along which heavier rails were laid in 1845 to support steam locomotives. The Murk Esk is crossed on a steel footbridge, beyond which the way heads towards old miners' cottages at Esk Valley. *(The local mines were ironstone and whinstone.) Notice an old North Eastern Railway trespass sign by the trackside.*

The path now draws alongside the present North York Moors railway line; *there are several unrenovated old engines and carriages on sidings here, looking distinctly forlorn.* Turn L on a well signed path uphill to a superb viewpoint above Grosmont, provided with a wooden bench. *The village lies at the confluence of the Murk Esk and Esk rivers.* Turn R down a track, then L through a gate, keeping to the L of the church and passing the village school. *The original horse-drawn carriages used the smaller, turreted tunnel which was blasted through high ground, as the deep river gorge offered no passage into the Murk Esk valley. At the far end, visitors are able to view the Engine Shed; a footbridge leads to the present-day station across the road.*

Grosmont Station - northern terminus of the North York Moors Railway

Grosmont comes alive during the summer season as holiday makers and steam-train enthusiasts throng its little streets. For walkers on Alfred Wainwright's Coast to Coast Walk, from St. Bees in Cumbria to Robin Hood's Bay, Grosmont represents the start of the last stage over low moorland to the North Sea.

The return leg to Goathland can be made by train - services run from April to October (about 3 per day), with greater frequency during June, July and August (about 7 per day). However, the walk back is over new ground to the E of the Murk Esk, with very good views.

Walk E up Grosmont's main street and after 200m take a path R opposite impressive Park Villa. The path drops through Crag Cliff Wood and down over 2 footbridges spanning feeder streams. Climb up to a lane and turn L. After 50m, it is worth climbing a bank to take a look at the Murk Esk precipitously below. Keep ahead along the lane, through a gate, and 15m after turn R on a paved way (a signed footpath) which contours along a field edge. Pass over a stile into lovely deciduous woodland (still Crag Cliff Wood) and ascend steadily on a good path alongside the causeway.

The path drops to cross a footbridge (ignore faint trods off R) and emerges at a field edge. Keep ahead along 2 fields, with fence and wood on the R. Cross a stile, go through a corner of wood, cross another stile and continue with woods now on the L. The path becomes muddier as it enters trees, a stream is crossed and a grassy bank climbed to a lane. Turn L through a metal gate, and at Green End take a L fork over a stile, through a gate and L onto a stony track. After 25m, turn R through a second farmyard and through a metal gate along a grassy way, keeping a hedge to the R.

At a track, go ½-L up through a reedy field, pass through a gate and turn R on the public road. Very soon, opposite Hollin Garth farmhouse, a good track leaves L; we, however, take a thin path between the road and the track, over boggy ground towards bracken. The path follows a wall, with Goathland now visible ahead, becomes much wider and turns R down to Hill Farm.

Take a good track L (E) opposite the farm, over a stream, aiming for a small farm (Lins Farm) below trees. Keep above the farm buildings and join another track coming in from the L at a wooden bench. *It is a good spot above Eller Beck valley where the railway crosses the river, offering superb views of passing trains.* Descend on a path above the beck and cross a footbridge beneath the railway bridge, where the fast-flowing waters below are channeled narrowly through a bed of rocks.

There are more excellent railway views from the steep climb up steps (bench ½ way up!), after which we cross a stile and walk up a field, fence on L. Another stile leads into a narrow lane between high hedges, and yet another brings us to the public road, along which turn L, go forward over a crossroads and bear R back to Goathland village centre.

WALK 34 CAR PARK, FALLING FOSS -
SHEEP HOUSE RIGG -
WHINSTONE RIDGE -
NEWTON HOUSE PLANTATION -
MAY BECK - CAR PARK, FALLING FOSS

7 miles (11.2km) - 3½ to 4 hours - Moderate; middle section exposed in bad weather

This walk starts from the car park (map ref: 888 036), about ¾ mile (1.2km) south of Red Gate on the B1416 between Ruswarp and the A171. Drop down the track to Falling Foss and cross the footbridge to Midge Hall *(the old Keeper's Cottage and aptly named on a still summer's evening!),* in its woodland setting by the 30ft (9m) high waterfall.

Walk along the R side of May Beck and in 50m turn R up a broad farm track. Soon there are open views R, with Foss Farm ahead. Pass

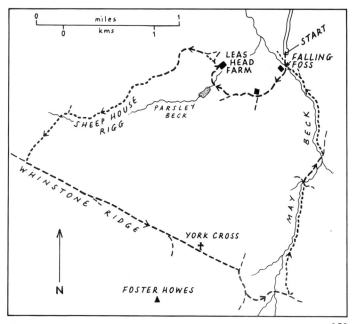

to the L of the buildings and through a gate. Beyond a L bend, turn R through a gate on a track undulating attractively along to Parsley Beck, which it crosses at a gate. Swing R to Leas Head Farm, go through the farmyard with its duckpond and turn sharp L through a gate and up a stony track. After about 50m, cut up L over grass to a large tree. Here, a gate leads to a stony field track which we climb, with good views developing to the North Sea between a shallow fold of hills, as well as over the wooded Littlebeck valley.

Pass a gate and continue climbing gradually round L on the old Leas Head Road. *At the next gate, a signpost points to Grosmont, an ancient route over Sleights Moor past High and Low Bride Stones.* Our way proceeds along field tops in delightful pastoral scenery. After the following gate, aim straight across open pasture towards a gate and post in the L corner ahead, meeting a wire fence to the L.

The track now emerges onto Sheep House Rigg in bracken and veers slightly L, thereafter contouring along rough slopes parallel to Parsley Beck. It soon climbs a little over heather, electricity pylons and traffic on the A169 conspicuous ahead.

Eventually, a path trends L to cross the head of Parsley Beck near a corner of Newton House Plantation. Here, keep SW on a path over rough heather moor, marked by a line of posts and passing beneath the power cables. At the final rising edge of moor are 2 inscribed stones, the left one dated 1784, and a clear track running along the Whinstone Ridge.

The Whinstone Ridge is an almost ruler-straight intrusion of basalt - a lava flow from 58 million years ago, sometimes referred to as the Cleveland Dyke. Stretching across the moors between Eskdale and Fylingdales Moor, this hard rock has been quarried for road building, in places - such as Great Ayton and Sil Howe - quite extensively.

Turn L (SE) along the moorland track, passing a deep, elongated trench R, one of several disused whinstone quarries hereabouts. Once under the power cables again and through a gate, the edge of Newton House Plantation draws nearer. Foster Howes lie up to the R, but our way keeps L over the shoulder of York Cross Rigg. After track and forest edge almost touch, we climb ahead with wide views in all directions, forking L just below the brow of the hill at a cairn. *(The right fork goes south-east along Foster Howes Rigg to Ann's Cross, Louven Howe and Lilla Howe.)*

In 200m, York Cross is reached, no longer a major landmark, but a stump in a stone plinth. The track drops towards the forest edge, disused whinstone quarries ahead on Pike Hill unplanted by the Forestry Commission. Go down a broad ride and at a forest road, turn

154

The remains of York Cross above Newton House Plantation

R. Fork L at the next junction and drop over May Beck, climbing past a pond L. In about 100m, turn L down a ride, ignore an overgrown R fork and keep L down a clear track.

The route soon reaches more open surroundings above May Beck's overgrown little valley, dropping very prettily to stream level. Cross a stile at a gate, over the beck and up, turning R on a stony road down to the Forestry Commission's May Beck car park and picnic area.

Go over the bridge and turn immediately L by a red waymarking post. Walk ahead over grassy levels, climb a bank under old oaks and continue along the well walked riverside trail. *The woodland contains fine examples of many deciduous tree species.*

Provided it is not very wet weather, keep L at a path junction and cross a shallow bend in May Beck on boulders, to arrive back at Midge Hall, whereupon turn R over the bridge and up to the car park. If the beck is full, keep R at the path junction, taking a higher line through woods back to the car park.

WALK 35 ROBIN HOOD'S BAY -
BOGGLE HOLE - STOUPE BROW -
DISMANTLED RAILWAY -
ROBIN HOOD'S BAY

5½ miles (9km) - 3 to 3½ hours - Moderate with some steep climbs

Robin Hood's Bay, known locally as 'Bay Town', is not thought to have any connections with the famous outlaw of Sherwood Forest, only becoming established much later in the early 16th century. A thriving and important fishing village by the 19th century, Bay Town's architecture remains virtually unchanged, a fascinating evocation of a past era when a fleet of some 40 boats (mostly sharp-prowed, flat-bottomed 'cobles' of Viking derivation) worked from the little port.

The Scarborough to Whitby railway came in 1885, and with it new markets for fish and the beginnings of tourism. Although the line closed in 1965 (this walk and others use the old track bed), Bay Town has continued to attract visitors, who flock here to enjoy its steep, picturesque streets and the beautiful coastline to the north and south with its 'scars', marine life, seabirds and excellent walking.

Merchant shipping and organised smuggling also contributed to Bay Town's prosperity during the 18th and 19th centuries and many houses

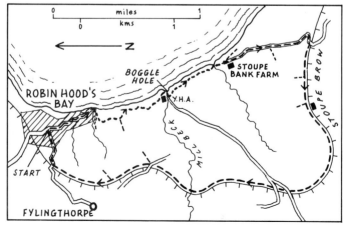

Robin Hood's Bay

contain features reflecting its seafaring tradition. As one would expect, there are today many shops, refreshment and eating places and a museum.

From the top car park *(vehicles are not allowed down into the lower town)*, pass a memorial to the famous lifeboat rescue of 1881 and walk steeply downhill towards the sea. Turn R into Albion Street (signed 'Cliff Path') and climb the steps. *(Alternatively, should the tide be low, our first destination - Boggle Hole - can be reached along the shoreline.)*

A plaque on an old stone notes the origins of this way, and a deviation right leads off into Marnar Dale Wildflower Reserve. Go up the stone then wooden steps and walkways, with fine views back to the red-roofed huddle of Bay Town and the boulder-clay cliffs beyond. Past Farsyde Stud and Riding Centre on the R, the path lies along duckboarding over eroded sections and passes a World War II bunker. Dropping steeply to wooded Mill Beck, we reach Boggle Hole youth hostel and field centre, once the old water mill. Cross the footbridge and turn R up the lane, watching for stone steps and a 'Cleveland Way' sign a few metres up on the L.

A climb now ensues to the cliff tops outside a fence, whereafter the path drops steeply again to cross a bridge over Stoupe Beck. *There are excellent views on the descent of cliffs ahead at Ravenscar.* Bear R up by a fence on paving slabs alongside a very muddy bridleway, climbing

157

steeply to Stoupe Bank Farm and a metalled lane. Walk ahead up this, past a Cleveland Way sign L, and prepare to gain the height lost descending from the top of Robin Hood's Bay!

The lane climbs relentlessly for ½ mile (.75km) and a stiff pull up round a bend leads to the cinder track bed of the old Scarborough to Whitby railway on Stoupe Brow, now a 'Permitted Path' *(but not an official right-of-way)*. Turn R under the bridge, enjoying the reward of easy walking for the remainder of the route!

The track makes a big loop, past Browside Farm, over embankments at Allison Head Wood and under Bridge Holm Lane (the road leading to Boggle Hole). 200m farther on, steps down and up take walkers over another road, followed by a picnic area near the one-time halt and an inhabited cottage. Thereafter, the walking is straightforward, at one point under an arch of alder trees, descending over Middlewood Lane, passing a caravan site L and becoming more pastoral towards Fylingthorpe. Turn R at the road to Robin Hood's Bay, pass the church and arrive back at the top car park.

A traditional Yorkshire 'Cobble'

WALK 36 RAVENSCAR - STOUPEBROW COTTAGE
FARM - DISMANTLED RAILWAY
-RAVENSCAR

4½ miles (7km) - 2 hours - Easy to moderate

Ravenscar was at one time earmarked for development as a resort on the scale of Scarborough, but the unstable nature of the clifftop site deterred all but the start of building. There are several places of refreshment to cater for the visitor, including the grandiose Raven Hall Hotel, finishing point for walkers on the 40-mile (64km) Lyke Wake Walk over the moors from Scarth Wood Moor, Osmotherley (see Chapter 5 on Long-distance and Challenge walks). The hotel was built in 1774 on the site of a Roman Signal Station atop 600ft (182m) cliffs - a magnificent vantage point now as then - the hall and gardens having been extended by the Willis family in the early 19th century.

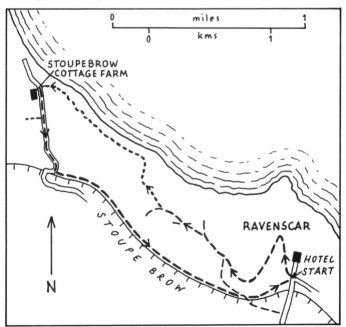

Ravenscar across Robin Hood's Bay

To the west of the village are extensive alum quarries. From the 17th to 19th centuries, alum was employed as a fixing agent for textile dyes and to cure animal hides. The process of making alum involved urine, brought here in barrel loads from London pubs! Readers wishing to explore the quarries, as well as the cliffs and shoreline which are of special interest for their rock formations and wild-life, can follow a waymarked Geological Trail. It starts at the National Trust Information Centre, up from the car park, from where an accompanying booklet can be obtained, along with much other useful material.

This route starts at the car park near the hotel. Walk up to the junction by the National Trust Centre and turn sharp R down a track signed 'To the Beach', descending past the castellated hotel walls and doubling back L across a golf course. *(A R turn from the corner leads steeply down to the shore.)*

Between 2 cattle-grids, the track veers R across a stream, with good views ahead of Robin Hood's Bay, and meets the Cleveland Way path coming down from the L. Keep L at the next fork and continue ahead through fields, branching R at a large stone and sign. Cross a stile and

160

walk along by a fence, with increasingly open views back to the high, collapsing cliffs below Ravenscar.

Erosion on the Yorkshire coast is, in fact, a serious problem. It is estimated that an average of 2" (5cm) per annum (or 20" - 50cm - per decade) is lost to the sea, accounting for an alarming amount of land and property which has disappeared in recent history. The big sea wall at Bay Town (Robin Hood's Bay), finished in 1975, is an attempt to stabilise the cliffs and protect this well-loved village from further damage.

At the next stile, turn R down the field edge, over the bottom stile and L along the clifftops. Eventually, the undulating path passes a World War II bunker and reaches the public road at Stoupebrow Cottage Farm. Loins need to be girded up here as we turn L for a rather relentless 200ft (61m) climb to Stoupe Brow. *The track bed of the old Whitby to Scarborough railway was engineered by John Waddell and opened in 1885: the line closed in 1965.*

Rounding a bend in the road, turn L onto the cinder track bed at the bridge, to enjoy pleasant easy walking for the remainder of the route. *Running midway between sea level and moor top, there are continuous sea and coastal views from the line. The gradient is gently uphill -hardly noticeable to the walker, but considerable for a railway: over the 5 miles from Bay Town to Ravenscar, it climbs 431ft (131m). Here and there, subsidence interrupts the surface, graphically illustrating the area's unstable geology.*

Wild flowers and shrubs have colonised the banks, including broom, whose black seed pods crack open audibly to disperse their contents on warm summer days. Farther on, the quarry is reached, originally opened in 1615 to extract and process the mineral alum contained in the grey shale. An ironstone seam, though of good quality, was too thin for profitable working.

Pass beneath a bridge, through a gateway and turn R onto a brick built track (the course of the Cleveland Way again) which climbs to the National Trust Centre and the road, just above the car park.

WALK 37 CHAPEL FARM - JUGGER HOWE BECK - HIGH MOOR - LILLA HOWE & CROSS - BROWN HILL - HARWOOD DALE MOOR - CHAPEL FARM

10½ miles (16.7km) - 5 hours - Moderate: boggy in places and exposed in bad weather

The walk starts from Chapel Farm, 1¾ miles (2.8km) NW of Harwood Dale. From Chapel Farm *(at the time of writing, 'Rosalie's Coffee House')*, take the Public Bridleway W towards 'Lilla' (Howe). The lane passes through a gate and down a field edge. At the bottom, turn R through a gate and go down a wooded pathway, crossing Lownorth Beck on a substantial railway-sleeper bridge.

After a short distance up through bracken, pass an arrowed turning R, bearing L instead and continuing up the muddy bridleway to a gate. This leads out into an open field: turn R and contour along above trees - liberally waymarked with yellow paint - and climb gradually to the renovated house at Park Hill. Pass behind the house, go over a stile and cross the track, and continue walking straight ahead along 2 field edges. Climb to a stile and descend to cross Bloody Beck.

We now ignore yellow arrows R, and walk L (NW) up Jugger Howe Beck. The going underfoot is pleasant at first, but deteriorates and can be very boggy. After a mile or so, the beck swings N and the buildings of Grouse Hill campsite come into view. Pass the eroded scar of the Lyke Wake Walk climbing R (NE) over Jugger Howe Moor. Almost immediately turn L (W) to mount High Moor on this same heavily used path, which becomes a muddy morass in wet weather.

Burn Howe is passed *('Howes' are the Bronze Age burial places of more important people, usually sited on high ground and appearing as low mounds)* and 1½ miles (2.4km) ahead stands the guidepost on Louven Howe, clearly visible in good weather. A broad track is joined near Burn Howe Duck Pond (not the first place you'd look for one!) and a mental note can be made of this spot (map ref: 898 991), as the return leg of this walk diverges off L here.

To visit Lilla Howe, now only ½ mile (800m) distant, either continue ahead to the guidepost and turn L (S) on the clear track, or short-cut the track corner SW from a cairn on a clear path.

Lilla Cross, temporarily removed to another site when this area was used for military training, but now in place again, is the oldest of all North York Moors crosses. It stands above the Bronze Age howe wherein was buried

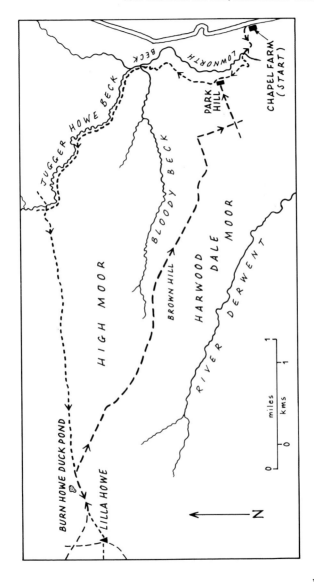

On the Lyke Wake path above Jugger Howe Beck

Lilla, minister to King Edwin, whose attempt to protect his king from assassination resulted in his own death in 626AD. The howe yielded gold and silver jewellery and ornaments and some filigree work.

Retrace steps to the point just E of Burn Howe Duck Pond and fork R (SE) on a clear track over moorland, past grouse butts and dropping gently to reach a gate into an enclosed field. Skirting Brown Hill, continue through another gate and on past another duckpond (not marked on maps). *Views are opening up to the right over the infant Derwent and Harwood Dale, with Langdale Rigg End a prominent feature due south.*

The track rises slightly to Pike Rigg. Go through a gate and pass a large green storage tank on breezeblocks, whereafter take the 2nd metal gate L and drop down with a fence on the L past a red marker and through a handgate at the bottom. We are now on a stony track near the triangular top of a plantation. Turn R downhill, then L down past another small plantation, keeping straight on, through a gate to Park Hill. From here, retrace the outward route over Lownorth Beck and back to the road at Chapel Farm.

NOTE: A much shorter walk in the valley of Lownorth Beck, avoiding all the moorland section, follows the start as far as the railway-sleeper bridge. Here, turn R on a narrow path before entering the woods proper: it stays close to Lownorth Beck, on the west bank. Just before its confluence with Bloody Beck, don't go through the gate ahead, but climb L up a small valley, over a stile and L again, now proceeding back S with a fence to the L.

Another stile is crossed and the way passes behind Park Hill house, thereafter along in a field above trees (no trod for a short distance). At a gate at the top of a bridleway, go downhill through trees to the railway-sleeper bridge and back to the road at Chapel Farm.

Distance: 2½ miles (4.25km) - 1½ hours - mostly easy.

WALK 38 GOATHLAND - TWO HOWES RIGG - SIMON HOWE - WHEELDALE BRIDGE - ROMAN ROAD - WEST BECK AND MALLYAN SPOUT - GOATHLAND

9½ miles (15.2km) - 4½ to 5 hours - Moderate: first part exposed in bad weather

Goathland is a popular destination for visitors to the North York Moors, for in addition to its Historical Railway Trail and its station on the North Yorks Moors Railway, the surrounding moors hold much of interest to the walker. (see also Walk 33)

From the road junction opposite the Mallyan Hotel at the SW corner of Goathland, walk up a sloping grassy path past a bench, angling away L from the road. There are one or two other paths in the bracken, but keep ahead, veering S and aiming for the highest visible ground (Two Howes Rigg). Topping a rise, The Tarn comes into view R, and our rather indistinct bridleway reaches a ruin near its shore -Old Kit Bield. *('Bields' are dry stone walled enclosures put up as*

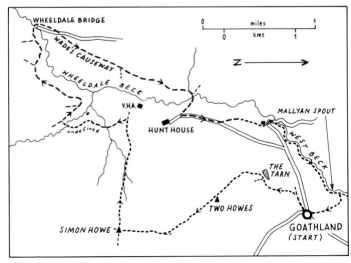

Fylingdales Early Warning Station from Simon Howe

protection for sheep in adverse weather. On windy days, they are of equal value to walkers!)

A right-of-way from here is shown turning up L (S) and, indeed, a thin trod does follow it through heather to Two Howes. Alternatively, continue along The Tarn's S bank and swing L up by its feeder stream. The 2 paths meet just by Two Howes, each mound topped by a cairn and incongruously juxtaposed in line of sight with the 'golf balls' of Fylingdales Early Warning Station.

'Howes' such as these - and there are over 3000 scattered over the North York Moors - are burial places, or barrows, of important people from the Middle Bronze Age. They are often found on ridges and watersheds, but the majority were ransacked by grave-robbers for what treasures they contained and sold to Victorian collectors with no record kept. Some, however, escaped and have yielded valuable data on burial customs of the time.

Our route passes close to the westernmost howe and, in about 20m, forks L. The well-walked, peaty path keeps to the broad crest of Two Howes Rigg, marked by occasional cairns. At a fork (with cairn), keep R towards Simon Howe, now close ahead, and climb up to it. A large cairn is surrounded by a ring of small standing stones, and nearby

167

to the NE stands and O.S. trig. point at 853ft (260m).

We are standing on the Lyke Wake Walk too, easily distinguished as an eroded scar across the moor - east towards Fylingdales and west to Wheeldale Beck, our way for almost a mile (1.5km). As usual with paths receiving heavy usage, the main trod becomes too deeply grooved for comfort, acts as a water channel, and is progressively ignored as flanking paths are established. The erosion process is common to all our well known walking routes, the Lyke Wake being just one graphic example among many. (For further details about the Lyke Wake Walk, please refer to Chapter 5.)

Walking W, Howl Moor Dike stream is followed down for a while, before it veers off L. Suddenly, Hunt House Crag is reached and the path begins dropping steeply towards Wheeldale Beck, with the youth hostel a short distance along to the R. A few metres down, take a track L, climbing back to the moor edge and swinging round L to contour through heather.

The double-rutted track aims for the upper corner of forest ahead and soon bends R towards an old nissen hut and ruined shepherd's shelter (John O'Groats), where it peters out. Bear L here along the top edge of bracken above Blawath Beck, then angle gradually down through it towards a stile into forest by a large rock slab. Cross the beck at the slab, and once in the plantation, walk up the narrow ride ahead, turning R onto a forest track. At a junction with a broad gravel road, keep forward downhill, swinging L round Gale Hill Point. Ignore turnings off, and in just under a mile emerge at the roadhead and open moor at Wheeldale Bridge. Cross Wheeldale Beck on the metal footbridge and walk alongside Sod Fold Slack, before crossing it too and walking up the course of the Roman Road. Cross the public road and a stile, at a footpath sign and information board.

Wade's Causeway is one of Britain's best preserved stretches of road from Roman times, running north-east from Cawthorn Camp. It formed part of a road connecting the fort at Malton with Whitby and the coastal signal stations. Here, where it has been excavated, the road's foundations are clearly revealed, complete with side drains. Originally, the top surface would have been fine stones or gravel.

In the interests of posterity and of walking comfort, it is probably best to walk alongside the actual roadway, which is very roughly paved and rises a foot or two (about 40cms) above the moor level. *As another sign tells us, the Roman Road belongs to HM the Queen, through the Duchy of Lancaster: the Ministry of Works has been given custody of this remarkable ancient monument.*

Continue forward through a wall gate and downhill through another

Mallyan Spout

gate and alongside a wall. A further gate leads down a grassy bank past 2 trees and down to Hazel Head Woods at Wheeldale Gill. Cross the footbridge and turn sharp R, ascending to meet the metalled Hunt House Road at parking space.

Turn L along the tarmac and in about 500m, just before the road bends R, fork off L down a good grassy track through bracken. At a gate, turn R alongside a wall and where it bends L, keep ahead in the same direction towards a red-roofed building. Pass its R side and go through a gate onto the public road, turning L down round a sharp bend. Just before the road bridge over West Beck, turn R by a white fence onto a public footpath.

The walk now follows the dramatic West Beck gorge, one of several post-glacial river channels in the region - narrow, rocky ravines which contain fast-flowing, bouldery streams, waterfalls and inaccessible woods. The scrambly path rises and falls in the gorge's exciting confines. Progress, predictably, can be slow, especially in wet weather or if the beck is in spate. Once a stile is passed, however, most of the ankle-twisting terrain is behind and the path levels off through trees. One tricky section remains, where the path climbs R up steps past a badly eroded section. At the time of writing, the path is still falling away and may well need to be re-routed again, so care is needed here.

Suddenly, the 70ft (21m) plume of Mallyan Spout is ahead, cascading over a rocky lip in the wooded ravine. *In dry spells, the volume of water may disappoint, but at such times the stream bed is more accessible by way of compensation. There are other cascades near Goathland - Water Ark Foss, Thomason Foss and Nelly Ayre Foss.*

The way climbs behind the waterfall, and after a little more rock-hopping arrives at a sign, whereupon we turn R on a well maintained and popular path up to Goathland's Mallyan Hotel and the start.

Wheeldale Lodge Youth Hostel

WALK 39   LEVISHAM - FARWATH - NEWTON DALE - LEVISHAM STATION - LEVISHAM

5¼ miles (8.5km) - 2½ hours - Moderate

Levisham is a village of broad grassy verges grazed by geese and lined with attractive cottages and farmhouses. There is also a Post Office and general store and a pub - the Horseshoe Inn - which serves good food. If parking space is to be chosen here, take care not to obstruct private access or passing vehicles in the one street.

This walk starts S from the village, on the road towards Lockton. Below the steep hairpin bend, take a wide bridleway off R (not the track off the apex of the bend itself). In about 150m, branch L at a junction on a grassy track down past the sadly abandoned and boarded-up church *(which is said to contain some interesting pre-Conquest carvings, its surroundings now overgrown)*.

Cross Levisham Beck by footbridge, go R along its bank and in a few metres pass through a gate and up a track. In 100m, turn R onto another track and follow its delightful course between old hawthorn trees, gently downhill, muddy in places, and into woods, contouring

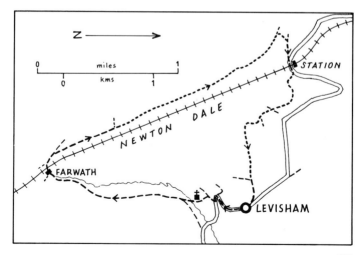

Levisham Station, North York Moors Railway

along above the beck. Emerging into open pasture, turn R through a gate and go along by the beck on a good track, aiming for the buildings of Farwath by the railway line.

Cross the line and beck by footbridge, turn R on a broad track and in about 100m, fork R. This rather unpromisingly boggy track (appropriately called Bottoms Road!) passes a conifer plantation R and rapidly improves to pleasant grassy going. *There are very few glimpses of the railway at this point - frustrating if a train happens to come along - but there is better to come!*

172

The track narrows to a path, overgrown in places, and we pass through several gates, gradually starting to climb across pasture. After 2 fields, the path deteriorates and is spoiled by bracken and undergrowth through East Brow Wood, especially in high summer. However, more ascent leads us into open country.

Walk uphill on the now clear path, parallel with a power line, then passing under it. Go through a gate and pass beneath a telegraph wire. ½-way across this well-grazed field, turn sharp R down the middle, into a shallow, gorsey depression and onto a clear footpath. *Views here are excellent. Newton Dale was scoured out by the force of water escaping from the ice-blocked lake which filled Eskdale to the north at the end of the last Ice Age 12,000 years ago.*

The narrow gorge runs from the head of the Murk Esk valley to the Vale of Pickering and was used by George Stephenson for the course of his Pickering to Whitby railway line, opened in 1836 (see Walk 33). Closed by Dr. Beeching in 1964, the line has been resurrected and is now operated by an independent trust. The North York Moors Railway runs from Easter to the end of october and at Christmas, though services are more frequent during the popular summer months. It is a fine and romantic sight to watch steam-drawn trains snake through the steep sided gorges of Newton Dale, and equally absorbing to take a ride in one. Just below our present position is Levisham Station, the first halt north of Pickering, where trains can be caught going north or south.

Descend the clear track through trees, cross the footbridge, and beyond a gate meet the public road. Go ahead to the station, cross the railway line and continue on the road, turning R past a cattle grid onto a footpath. We now cross a stream, go through a gate and ascend a particularly attractive path in quite exquisite woodland. Past another gate, walk up a field edge towards corrugated-iron huts. Here, bear R to a stile and turn R up a very pleasant grassy path, climbing diagonally at a gentle gradient, with marvellous valley views and drifts of foxgloves below.

The path levels off at another superlative viewpoint by a wooden bench. Keep R in front of it, ignoring the hollow way to the L, and contour narrowly and entertainingly round the head of Keldgate Slack. Climbing to a gate, the route thereafter keeps L along a field edge by a wall, crosses a stile and another field, before reaching a lane which leads ahead to the top end of Levisham village.

WALK 40 CAR PARK, HORCUM DIKE -
LEVISHAM MOOR - DUNDALE GRIFF -
HOLE OF HORCUM -
CAR PARK, HORCUM DIKE

5¼ miles (8.5km) - 2½ hours - Moderate

From the car park on the A169 above the Hole of Horcum (between Pickering and Whitby), walk N on the verge and, right on the hairpin bend, go through a gate/stile onto a good stony track. (Make sure not to take one of the other paths L and R.) *There are clear views, both of Fylingdales Ballistic Missile Early Warning Station back to the NE, and into the Hole of Horcum.*

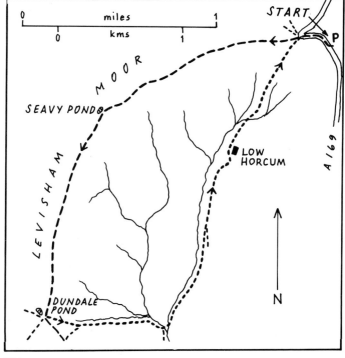

Approaching the Hole of Horcum

In a short distance, a brass plaque by the wayside announces, 'Levisham Estate. This land is owned by the National Parks Commission and you are welcome to walk here. Please note that vehicles, metal detectors, guns, fires and tents are not allowed on the moor...' (such notices fire the imagination by what they omit!)

The easy track gradually veers more southerly past Seavy Pond, with views into the Hole becoming obscured by intervening Broadhead, Sheephouse and Horness Riggs. *Levisham Moor itself, however, is rich in ancient sites. One such is an Iron Age Dike stretching west towards West Side Brow. A plaque tells us it was probably a territorial boundary constructed 2000 years ago; the earthworks associated with a fortified farmstead of similar date are not easy to make out, though the dike is a conspicuous feature.*

Farther south, at Dundale Pond, another information plate reads, 'This small valley was given to the monks of Malton Priory in about 1230 as pasture for their sheep, cattle and horses. Dundale Pond was probably made at this time as a place for stock to drink'.

Here we turn down L into Dundale Griff and follow the 1st part of Walk 41 (which actually begins ¾ mile (1.2km) away in Levisham), through the sensational Hole of Horcum and back to the A169 and the start of the walk.

WALK 41   LEVISHAM - DUNDALE GRIFF - HOLE OF HORCUM - SALTERGATE BROW - NEWGATE BROW - BRIDESTONES - STAIN DALE - LOCKTON - LEVISHAM

12 miles (19.5km) - 5 to 6 hours - Moderate

Levisham, with its halt on the North York Moors Railway a mile to the west in Newton Dale, is approached by road from the A169 via Lockton and a 1 in 3 hairpin. Though somewhat isolated, it is a pleasant, timeless place, with broad grassy verges backed by pretty cottages and farmhouses. There is also a small store and Post Office, and an hospitable pub, the Horseshoe Inn, at the top of the only street.

Car parking space in the village should be chosen with care so as not to block access or obstruct passing vehicles, including tractors. This walk is notable for the many features of interest it takes in and for the variety of terrain and scenery covered.

From the village's N end, fork R past the Post Office and walk up the metalled Limpsey Gate Lane, a cul-de-sac for motors. It becomes rougher and drops to a stile and gate, whereafter we cut down ½-R over cropped turf and on through bracken to join the main path down Dundale Griff, keeping to the R of trees and the usually dry stream bed. *('Griff' is the local term for side-valley.)*

The way drops interestingly into a densely wooded fold of small hills where Pigtrough, Dundale and Water griffs meet. At a sign, turn L, cross Dundale Beck *(now showing signs of life!)* on stepping stones and Levisham Beck on a plank bridge. The path now continues between beck and wall, and soon exciting views open out ahead of the hillsides enclosing the Hole of Horcum. We leave the wooded confines of Horcum Slack, cross a stile and emerge onto grassy slopes. Keep up R to join the higher path by 2 small trees and pass a wooden post.

When the buildings of Low Horcum are in view, the extraordinary, scalloped, hollowed flanks of the Hole are seen to best advantage, though there are equally fine views from its rim. *Legendary home of the giant Horcum, the huge natural hollow was excavated, along with nearby Newton Dale, by water escaping from the ice-dammed lake which filled Eskdale 12,000 years ago at the end of the last Ice Age. it is crossed by walkers on the Cleveland Way 'Missing Link' and the North York Moors*

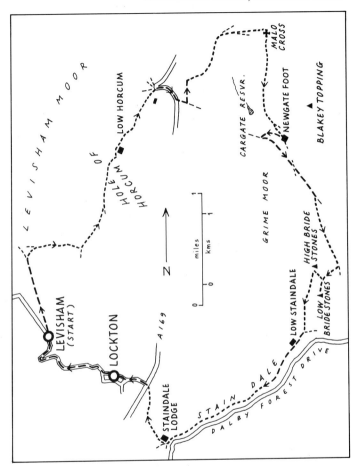

Crosses Walk, as well as being a popular spot for hang-gliders and model aircraft enthusiasts.

Low Horcum, a long while uninhabited and surrounded by thistles and the remains of a one-time garden, is being renovated at the time of writing. Go round L of the house and continue forward over grass, dropping across a stile and a feeder stream of Levisham Beck. Climb on in low bracken and aim for the obvious track up the shoulder of the valley

Malo Cross

head. The path runs up in an eroded groove above High Horcum, of which little is seen, crosses a stile and reaches the A169 at a hairpin bend.

Suddenly, Fylingdales Ballistic Missile Early Warning Station is close by above a rim of moor, while to the west lies the Newton Dale gorge. Walk R up the road, past a large barn L, with good views into the Hole of Horcum. In about 100m, turn L on a metalled lane signed 'Public Bridleway'. Go through the white gate ahead (Private Road to Newgate Foot Farm) and turn L on a stony track along the edge of a conifer plantation. In about 350m, go through a gate and turn R over well cropped, springy turf along Saltergate Brow.

Fylingdales' familiar 'golf balls' are in clear view, as the old grassy track

Fylingdales Early Warning Station from Saltergate Brow

keeps to the bank edge. Radar installations inside the 160ft (49m) high fibreglass radomes watch over a 3000 mile span between Turkey and the Arctic. 2 similar stations exist, one at Clear in Alaska, the other at Thule in Greenland. It is said that the 'golf balls' here are to be replaced by a huge pyramid, thus changing for good the geometry of this famous landmark! Also from here, the A169 appears as a fragile channel of communication undulating across heather moorland.

Continue on round Saltergate Brow, ignorning a track off L as the bank swings E. Shortly afterwards, drop gently down a grassy track through bracken to the edge of forest and the ancient inscribed stone of Malo Cross.

From here, veer R (S) and follow a well walked path away from the forest edge itself. *There is a dramatic sighting of Blakey Topping to the L - a kind of smoothed-off, cosmeticised clone of Roseberry Topping near Guisborough!* Beyond a gate, the way contours over broad pastureland, eventually descending to a gate and stile before rising directly towards Newgate Foot house. Cross another stile, turn R then R again up a concrete track. *(If desired, Blakey Topping can be climbed by turning L down the farm lane. In 400m at a track crossroads, go ½-L up through bracken to the heathery summit, a good viewpoint with the remains of an ancient stone circle.) The western section of Dalby Forest lies on the land like a deep-pile rug. Tiny Cargate Reservoir, hidden before, is visible on the right in its little valley at the bottom of Long (but short!) Gill.*

At the top of the concrete track, turn L by a 'National Trust Bride-

179

High Bride Stones

stones' sign, go through a gate onto Grime Moor and walk along a broad level track by fields, with far-reaching views in most directions. 50m before the track enters forest, go through a gate R, down the forest edge and through another gate at a 'Nature Reserve' sign. *Administered jointly by the National Trust and the Yorkshire Naturalists' Trust, Bridestones Moor and Dove Dale Woods enjoy concessionary public access, but care should be taken not to damage flora or stray from paths.*

Proceed ahead on a good path over heather and at the marshy top of Bridestone Griff, turn R at a National Trust sign. The well walked path winds through heather round to Low Bride Stones, a row of amazingly undercut and weathered sandstone outcrops. After looking at them, retrace steps for 200m and turn down L through bracken, over Bridestone Griff and up to High Bride Stones, equally fascinating with arches, holes and eroded ledges. *Many Bridestones exist on the North York Moors and it is likely that their naming is associated with ancient fertility rites.*

Our walk continues S down Needle Point, a sharp ridge between Dovedale and Bridestone griffs. Drop steeply, cross the stream and proceed along wooded Dove Dale. *These birch and native Scots pine are indiginous, surrounded by vast plantings of Forestry Commission conifers.* After turning L to recross the stream on a small footbridge and passing through a squeeze stile, turn sharp R back over the stream. *(About ½ mile, 1km, to the E along a good path lies Staindale Water, a small artificial lake with picnic areas, car park and WC.)*

A track now takes us SW to Low Staindale, which is passed below the buildings and a double stile climbed through a hawthorn hedge. A clear track leads on in riverside pasture beneath deciduous woods R. *Part of Dalby Forest Drive is just across Staindale Beck.* Cross a small footbridge with stiles and keep ahead in the same direction, aiming L of a telegraph pole by a small pumping station. Cross a stile and walk through Holm Wood, ending at a gate and over pasture by a large oak to some barns. Go through 2 more gates and round R in front of Staindale Lodge.

Keeping R, walk along the gravel drive, over a short stretch of grass, then through a gate into a mixed copse and along to the next gate. The way now establishes its ancient origins as we climb a sunken groove through delightful woods above Rustifhead Slack. 2 handgates later, open fields are reached by a wire fence and electricity pylons. Carry on ahead to a gate, cross the A169 and walk into Lockton *(shops, pub, youth hostel)*. Keep R down Mill Bank Road, past the erstwhile mill and up the 1 in 3 hairpin *(a real sting in the walk's tail!)* back to Levisham village.

NOTE: A much shorter itinerary dealing only with Levisham Moor and the Hole of Horcum can be followed by turning to Walk 40.

WALK 42 LANGDALE END - LANGDALE RIGG - BICKLEY TROD - BIRCH HALL FARM - LANGDALE END

6 miles (9.5km) - 3 hours - Moderate

*The Forestry Commission has been planting trees in the North York Moors -
mostly conifers which thrive on the poor soil and in exposed situations -since
its first acquisition of land north of Thornton Dale in 1920. Since then, its
role has been extended from simple timber production to include such diverse
activities as the management of wildlife habitats and the provision of
recreational facilities such as car parks, picnic areas and forest walking
trails.*

*18% of the National Park's area is forest-covered, up to a third of the
resulting timber going to provide pit-props for Yorkshire coal mines. The
majority of trees in Dalby Forest come from Wykeham Forest Nursery as 2
year old transplants and are placed 2m apart in deep furrows to encourage
healthy root growth. 6 to 8 years later, a thicket has formed, and from the
25th year onwards, at 6 or 7 year intervals the plantations are thinned to
increase the volume of the remaining trees. Only at around the 50th year of a
tree's life is economic maturity reached.*

*About 120 acres of mature Dalby Forest are felled and re-stocked each
year - a prodigious 20,000 tons of timber to be transported out.*

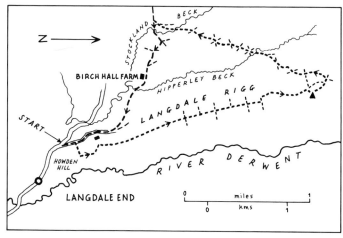

Low Dalby Visitor Centre

The Forestry Commission's Visitor Centre is at Low Dalby, reached by toll road north from Thornton Dale or south-west from Langdale End (starting point for this walk). The forestry village here was built in 1949, the Centre and forest offices being housed in converted farm buildings. As well as selling books, leaflets, maps and souvenirs, there is a fascinating exhibition of the Forestry Commission's work, and an imaginative visual display of forest wild-life, complete with recorded sound effects. Nearby refreshment kiosk, drinking water point, WC's, telephone and generous car parking complete an amenity which can form the base for a rewarding day or more's exploration.

In fact, short, colour-coded waymarked trails (mostly 1 to 3 miles, 1.5 to 5km in length) abound, particularly from Low Dalby itself and from points along the Dalby Forest Drive. Altogether there are some 75 miles (120km) of roads through the adjacent forest. Another very pleasant spot is Staindale Lake, about 3 miles (5km) to the north-east. Leaflets relating to the forest trails are obtainable from the Visitor Centre.

Langdale End is little more than a scattering of farmsteads strung out along the Bickley to Hackness 'B' road. Any roadside parking spot should be chosen carefully to avoid inconveniencing local residents and passing *traffic. Howden Hill is a conspicuous landmark and it is from the road junction on its south-west flank that this walk begins (map ref: 935 914).*

Fork R (N) and in 300m turn R through the 2nd gate, signed 'Public Footpath'. Walk to the field top and turn L, aiming towards the S end of Langdale Rigg. A gate in the field's top R corner leads out to a good track L which climbs the narrow ridge end above the River Derwent's gorge - a glacial meltwater channel from the last Ice Age.

Conifer plantings on the ridge obscure views *(though changes in tree cover do occur from time to time)*. From a gate, a forest ride is followed ahead (roughly N), picking up the 'Blue Man' waymarks of the Forest Trail from Reasty Bank to Allerston. Turn L then R and in about 500m a stile R leads to the OS pillar on Langdale Rigg End (802ft - 244m). *There are wide views N over Lownorth, Harwood Dale and Fylingdales Moors, in addition to many thousands of acres of Forestry Commission plantings.*

From the trig point, the trail is rejoined by dropping NW to a gate almost opposite a L turn (signed) which we take. This footpath ('Bickley Trod') threads through marvellous forest terrain for almost 2 miles (3km) in a generally SW direction, passing numerous intersections but confirmed by the Forest Trail waymarking. Cross Hipperley Beck on a footbridge, climb over Maw Rigg End, cross a forest road and drop down over Stockland Beck in its charming little valley.

300m further on in the same SW direction, a surfaced road is met: here we turn L and leave the Forest Trail. Keep R at Raven Scar, an open area after Stockland Beck is re-crossed, walk on past Birch Hall Farm (R) and follow the forest road over Hipperley Beck towards the end of Langdale Rigg and Howden Hill, whence the public road is joined down to Langdale End.

Young Roe Deer

WALK 43 REASTY BANK - WHISPER DALES - BROXA - RIVER DERWENT - BARNS CLIFF END - REASTY BANK

7¾ miles (12.5km) - 3½ to 4 hours - Moderate: one steep ascent (avoidable)

Reasty Bank is situated due south of Robin Hood's Bay and due west of Cloughton, not far from the village of Harwood Dale. At the bank top, on the Scalby to Harwood Dale 'B' road, the Forestry Commission has

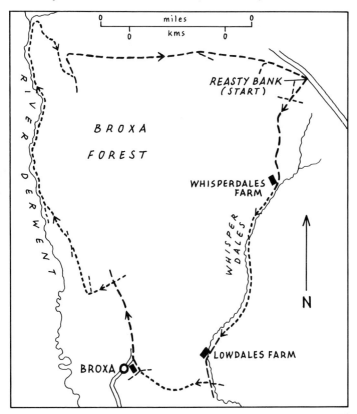

established a car park and picnic area.

West from here stretch vast tracts of woodland, providing waymarked walks, forest drives, nature trails, picnic sites and, at Low Dalby, a Forest Information Centre. (For more details, see Walk 42). Even in Broxa Forest alone, which this walk penetrates, there are miles of rough roads, rides and paths on which to wander in peace and solitude. (A large scale map and compass can be useful in such terrain.) The Forestry Commission has also set up a long-distance forest trail from Reasty Bank to Allerston (on the A170 near Thornton Dale). It is a 16 mile hike (26km) and waymarked with a Blue Man symbol. Walkers successfully completing the walk can purchase a special Blue Man badge.

From the car park on Reasty Bank, walk SW down a gravel road, past more parking places by forest rides. The track veers L and descends wooded Swinesgill Rigg, emerging into the open above Whisper Dales, an intimately pastoral landscape held between wooded hills.

Pass the entrance to Whisperdales Farm and keep ahead to the R of a small stream under a bank. The field track continues by the stream before crossing it and rising slightly onto a raised ledge between fields. Cross a field to a stile by another stream and proceed forward over grass, with Haggland Wood above L. Over more stiles, the grassy track leads on past hawthorn trees down to Lowdales Farm.

Cross 2 shallow fords by footbridge and keep L at a farm road junction, along a surfaced lane between high hedges. Just before a footbridge and bridleway sign L, turn R up an ancient hollow way in a tunnel of low, overhanging trees. When open woodland is reached, keep straight on as the path, paved in places, steadily climbs a small valley. At the top, it continues between hedges and reaches a gate at the corner of Broxa Farm.

Turn R alongside the farm complex and at the road junction, turn R towards the line of forest ahead on a metalled lane. Where it reaches the tree edge, turn L past a pole barrier on a path along the edge of forest, ignoring the 1st track *(though this would offer an easy return short-cut, avoiding the descent into, and subsequent ascent out of, the Derwent valley. The main route can be joined at Barns Cliff End)*.

The way now veers R and begins to drop, levelling off in delightful deciduous woodland before descending further to join a path by the River Derwent. Turn R, pass a footbridge L and a marker post, and walk ahead with the river on the L. The path is shady and secretive, twisting through mixed forest, a little boggy here and there but, as paths go, a real charmer!

Whisper Dales

Just beyond a metal footbridge where the Derwent and Harwood Dale Beck meet, the path swings R and climbs steeply into Hingles Wood. Ignore a path off R at a bench and continue to climb ahead. Levelling off, the path veers R and climbs, levelling off again through conifers and deeply covered with pine needles.

At a junction with a track, turn L uphill, emerging into a forest ride near a marker post. Here, turn R on a bracken-fringed path - the final pull up - to meet a stony forestry road on the top of Barns Cliff End. Turn L and in 200m there are marvellously open and wide-ranging views over the Derwent valley and the moors and forest to the west, made all the more vivid by having spent the last few miles walking in woods.

We now follow the forestry road round R (E), *past many splendid viewpoints to the north, including an aerial look over the old Low North Camp, overgrown with gorse, but its concrete roads and foundations still clear.* Keep L at a fork, then at a pole barrier turn L along the very broad forest road which leads straight back along the escarpment to the car park on Reasty Bank.

WALK 44 BRIDGE FARM - HAYBURN WYKE - LITTLE CLIFF - CLOUGHTON WYKE - DISMANTLED RAILWAY - BRIDGE FARM

6 miles (9.5km) - 3 to 4 hours - Moderate: care needed in wet or windy weather

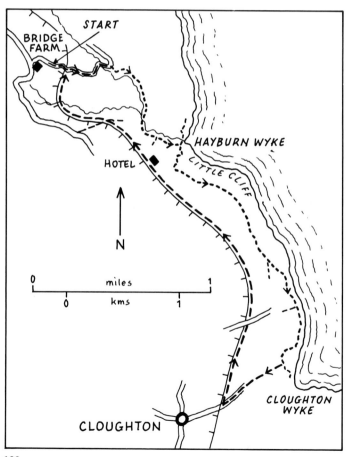

The walk begins from a lane east off the Staintondale to Cloughton B road (map ref: 997 978) near Bridge Farm and the dismantled Whitby to Scarborough railway line.

Walk along the lane towards the coast, past Lowfield campsite and down over a stream valley. At the far side, where the lane bends sharp L by a bungalow, turn R on a signed Public Bridleway which crosses a field and enters the edge of woods. Take the path R at a handgate, signed 'To Beach and Cliff'.

The way drops very attractively in trees down to Hayburn Beck, flowing between mossy boulders in a small, deeply wooded valley. The path undulates before crossing an airy footbridge, whereafter turn L (not R up steps) above the beck. We soon join a broader path, along which turn L to reach a Hayburn Wyke Nature Reserve sign and Cleveland Way post.

'Wyke' is a local word for a sheltered cove. The 34 acres of woodland backing Hayburn Wyke are managed by the Yorkshire Naturalists' Trust and, whilst access is unrestricted, the visiting public are asked not to pick flowers or damage plant life.

From the signboard, descend steps L, and just before the footbridge over Hayburn Wyke, turn R between rocks to arrive above the pebbly foreshore, reached by a scramble down R. *It is a delightful spot, in calm weather ideal for a picnic. There are fossils among the pebbles, while Hayburn Beck tumbles picturesquely over a lip of rocks in a small waterfall.*

Retrace steps to the signboard and turn L on the Cleveland Way, climbing through woodland which is ablaze with flowers such as celandines, anemones and bluebells in late spring. The way veers L above the tree and bush covered Little Cliff, and beyond Rodger Trod is squeezed less comfortably between agricultural land and the crumbling cliff edge. *Extra care is needed in places, especially in rough conditions.*

Before Cloughton Wyke, there are intermittent views down to inaccessible rocky beaches through a screen of blackthorn and furze. Where the path swings inland (SW) above Salt Pans, turn R onto the unenclosed farm lane towards Cloughton village, and when the Yorkshire Coast railway track bed is reached, turn R along it. *(A detour can be made to Cloughton Wyke, a popular place for sea angling, by following the cliff path a short distance further.)*

From now on, the walking is an easy, level stroll on a 'Permitted Path' *(not an official right-of-way)* following the old railway line. *Birch, scrub willow and other flora now fringe the wayside and there are*

Hayburn Wyke

marvellous sea views to the east. 2 miles (3.5km) and a couple of bridges later, the track crosses the wooded Hayburn Beck valley. About 300m beyond, leave it for the lane near Bridge Farm and the start of this walk.

WALK 45   WEST AND EAST AYTON - OSBORNE LODGE FARM - MOWTHORP BRIDGE - HACKNESS HALL - COCKRAH HOUSE - RIVER DERWENT - FORGE VALLEY - WEST AYTON

10 miles (16km) - 5 to 6 hours - Moderate

This walk can be taken in 2 separate halves, each with its own worth-while qualities and attractions. To complete the circuit of Forge Valley (4½ miles - 7km - mostly easy terrain), follow route directions as far as the road at Green Gate in Raincliffe Woods. Here turn L, and in about 500m cross the River Derwent on one of two footbridges to join the path back to West Ayton, as described towards the end of this walk.

To complete the Hackness circuit (5½ miles - 9km - moderate terrain), start from one of the small car parks on the road up Forge Valley, on the left as you approach the hill to Green Gate. From here, simply follow route directions, leaving them about 500m after entering the Forge Valley Nature Reserve, to cross L over the Derwent on one of two footbridges back to the road.

West and East Ayton are twin villages straddling the River Derwent on the A170 Pickering to Scarborough road. There is an impressive 14th

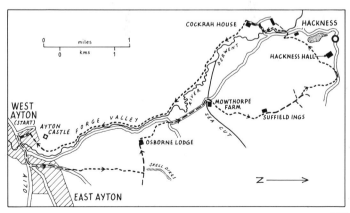

West Ayton 'castle'

century fortified tower at West Ayton - the remains of a 12th to 15th century manor house, while at East Ayton stands an interesting 13th century church.

From West Ayton, walk E, over the River Derwent and past the Forge Valley/Hackness road L. Just beyond the church, turn L onto the Scarborough road and immediately L again into Moor Lane. Follow this up past a housing estate into open country and at a 'Road Narrows' sign, take a good track L through woods.

Emerging from the trees, go slightly L and then forward on a track with a hedge R. (The start of this track was ploughed up at the author's last visit - possibly the same fate awaits the remainder, though it is a right-of-way.) The hopefully grassy track climbs gradually - where overgrown, take to the fields L. Pass a small plantation at the top and turn L past Skell Dikes *(a prehistoric boundary overgrown with hawthorn)* to Osborne Lodge Farm. *This distinctive collection of traditional farm buildings is completely unspoilt by modern development.*

Go through the farmyard past haystacks and through a gate into a field. Half way along, go through another gate L into trees on a narrow path downhill, becoming steeper before levelling off. Emerging from Raincliffe Woods, keep straight ahead to the road at Green Gate.

We now drop down Mowthorp Road, past neat bungalows to Mowthorp Bridge spanning Sea Cut. *This artificial drain takes excess water from the River Derwent east to the sea, its original course before*

The path through Greengate Wood

North Sea ice diverted it south during the last Ice Age.

Walk into Mowthorp Farm's entrance and ahead between barns through a metal gate. A grassy, hollow way flanked by hawthorn trees leads up to a white-painted gate with a yellow waymark. The right-of-way here continues for 100m alongside the conifer plantation before veering L uphill across a field to a gate in Hawthorn Wood. However, if planted, walk straight up the field edge and keep in single file in either case.

A continuation of the hollow way leads up through Hawthorn Wood, over a large fallen tree and out to a gate at a field corner. Turn

½-L along by a hedge to Suffield Ings Farm. 2 more gates take us to the R of the buildings and onto a broad, stony field track. Go forward and at a junction with a metalled lane, turn L, past the entrance to Suffield Heights, over a stile and onto a semi-surfaced track.

About 15m before the track swings R to a disused quarry at a 'Private Keep Out' sign, watch carefully for an indistinct path dropping L by a fence post into a bushy hollow. Follow it down into trees, past an impresssive old lime kiln and an ancient tree. The undergrowth diminishes, and beyond a handgate the route is the bed of a small dry valley down Greengate Wood.

At the bottom, cross a stile and walk L, slanting down grass to the road, about 750m E of Hackness village. *(If time allows, a short detour is worthwhile. St. Hilda of Whitby Abbey established a nunnery here in AD680, but even this out-of-the-way setting did not escape the Danish invasion of 867 in which it was destroyed. The village pond and an inscribed cross, now in the church, are all that remain of St. Hilda's nunnery, despite its rebuilding and occupation from the 11th century until the Dissolution.)*

At a footpath sign some 100m along the road, aim back up L onto an old track on a shallow ledge just below the wood boundary. This climbs gently round L, as the road swings away R, and rises to a stile. Ascending easily over pasture towards a line of trees, there are excellent views R down to Hackness Hall. *Designed by the architect John Carr of York, this stately Georgian manor was once the home of Lady Hoby, the first woman diarist: it now belongs to Lord Derwent.*

Levelling off then dropping, always just outside the woods, the path leads on above Hackness Lake to a conspicuous stile in a double wire fence. Contour along the pasture ahead, keeping above Mill Farm at first then dropping in a zig-zag to a stile and the road.

Cross the road, then the Derwent on a footbridge, turning L to follow the raised river bank fringed with gorse. Stay outside a wire fence and cross 2 small feeder streams at Wrench Green. Keep L along a field edge by the river, and at the road bridge turn R.

By Rose Cottage at the T-junction and cul-de-sac sign, turn L and walk past Cockrah House barns to a metal waymarked gate. Go through, but aim immediately L down to the bottom of hilly pasture. Keep R of a field end, then L past a stand of trees, after which the path climbs by a fence to a waymarked tree. Cross the fence (no stile) and stream, and continue ahead alongside the Derwent.

Soon, the footbridges of Weir Head are in view - *worth diverting to for a look at the start of the big Sea Cut drain. Hereafter, the Derwent is noticeably depleted, a mere shadow of its former self.* Waymarked stiles

In Forge Valley

and gates lead on over rough water-meadow. When the river meanders away L, keep straight on, past a marshy area R, towards the corner of wooded hill ahead. Here the river is rejoined at a stile and signboard announcing the Forge Valley Nature Reserve and telling us:

'Forge Valley woodland is a remnant of forest which covered much of Britain in prehistoric times. Despite much use by man, including forges after which it is named, it still retains many features of natural forest: alders in the wet valley bottom, mixed ash and elm on the flushed slopes, oaks on higher, drier ground - all characteristic of the soils they grow on. There is much rich plant and animal life.'

The notice reminds visitors not to collect specimens or carry out field work without permission. Those wishing to do so can find the appropriate addresses to apply to in this guide under 'Useful Addresses'.

The path continues alongside the Derwent in marvellous woods, mostly on duckboarding and passing 2 footbridges about 500m apart *(access to road and small car parks)*. Leave the Nature Reserve and pass a weir. When the strip of land ahead narrows between river and trees, keep to the field edge alongside trees. At the end, take the stony track ½-R to a gate. Follow the good track past the imposing ruined tower of Ayton Castle, go through a kissing gate and forward onto a road by houses. Turn L and drop to the A170 at West Ayton.

CHAPTER 5

LONG-DISTANCE AND CHALLENGE WALKS

Perhaps because the topography of the North York Moors is so varied and readily accessible, it provides ideal terrain for long-distance and challenge walks. There are at least 16 recognised routes (the total changes as walks become defunct or newly devised), ranging from 20 to 50 mile (32 to 80km) hikes which are completed at one go and will test the strongest walker, to longer itineraries most commonly taken in stages and lasting several days.

Some challenge walks are held as organised events, usually on an annual basis and embodying a spirit of competition, either between fellow walkers, or against the clock, or both. Provided rights-of-way are used throughout, there is nothing to stop walkers following any route at a more leisurely pace whenever the inclination to do so occurs.

Many long-distance walks have been conceived with specific themes in mind, linking features of interest (eg. The Crosses Walk or Seahorse Saunter). Of those not organised as annual events, some have time limits attached but can be attempted at any time; others still exist simply as routes to be enjoyed by whatever method fits the needs of individual walkers best.

Most of the walks are admirably described in booklets or leaflets on sale at bookshops or information centres, or obtainable from the organisers. Most are mentioned in *The Long Distance Walker's Handbook*, published by A. & C. Black Ltd. For this reason, only outline details of the walks are given in this chapter, some contributed by the originators themselves and appearing under their own names. The walks appear in alphabetical order.

THE BILSDALE CIRCUIT *by Mike Teanby*

The Bilsdale Circuit was first walked in April 1977 and in the next few years was to become a firm favourite with those seeking a realistic challenge on the North York Moors.

To devise a new route in an area packed with outstanding scenery and an existing network of footpaths was not easy, but Bilsdale with its adjacent ridges rising to 1000ft (305m) above sea level, provided a clue.

After an abortive winter recce, the first circuit was completed by David Chisman, Terry Kelly, Reg Rigby and myself on 3rd April 1977 from Doncaster, all members of the Long Distance Walkers Association. The walk encompassed the vast moorland ridges and included many miles of 'heather bashing', much compass work and a battle with the elements as persistent snow showers closed in during the latter part of the day's walking.

A few minor alterations to the route extended it to nearly 30 miles (48km), with approximately 4000ft (1219m) of ascent and only a minor amount of 'rough stuff'. There have been several organised events on the circuit by the L.D.W.A. North Yorkshire Group, who recognise a good walk when they tread one! The largest number of people attempting it at one go was 450, on behalf of Sue Ryder Homes, raising over £20,000 in sponsorship on that occasion.

The Bilsdale Circuit remains, however, the walk for small parties who, above all, enjoy getting off the beaten track into new wild environments and are able to dig into their physical and mental reserves to beat the challenge. Support teams can be used, but more often are not, and it is much more satisfying to carry all one needs for the day than rely on someone else to do things for you.

The circuit has been run, walked and crawled over, the latter as a 2-day expedition! One chap has even extended the route through Helmsley to give him a tough 50 miles (80km). Age is no barrier - old and young alike have trod its way at sometime or other.

In 1987, the circuit will be 10 years old and in this decade has attracted many thousands of walkers: there remain, however, few signs and stiles, and there is little or no evidence of them passing.

Next time you are examining the badges on a rucksack or sweater, look out for the tiny blue badge with gold edges and Bilsdale logo - you are looking at a discerning hiker who at sometime has completed a rather splendid moorland walk.

START AND FINISH: Newgate Bank car park, north of Helmsley (564 890).
LENGTH: 30 miles (48km)
DETAILS: s.a.e. to Mike Teanby, Bilsdale Circuit Recorder, Lyndhurst, Sutton Road, Thirsk, North Yorkshire. Also a booklet by Mike Teanby, *The Bilsdale Circuit,* published by Dalesman Books. Badge and certificate available on completion. No time limit.
OS MAPS: Sheet 100.

THE CLEVELAND WAY

This 93 mile (150km) footpath was opened in May 1969 after almost 16 years of planning, though the original idea for a long-distance walk over the Yorkshire moors and coast dates back half a century.

The Cleveland Way is a varied and interesting tramp which takes in a sizeable chunk of the best the North York Moors National Park has to offer from natural features such as heather moor, forest, lake and coastal scenery, to villages and farms, monuments and Bronze Age remains, ancient trackways and modern industry, sites of industrial archaeology, abbeys and fishing villages.

The waymarked route stays, for the most part, within the National Park, making a (usually) clockwise arc, often close to its boundary. it begins at Helmsley (on the A170 between Thirsk and Pickering), passing close to Rievaulx Abbey and reaching the escarpment edge at Sutton Bank Information Centre. A short detour to the Kilburn White Horse is followed by progress north along the escarpment past Gormire Lake, along the Hambleton Drove Road and down to Osmotherley.

The next section along the north-west scarp is often one of the hardest, with a switchback of climbs and descents traversing Scarth Wood Moor, Live Moor, Carlton Bank, Cringle Moor, Hasty Bank and Urra Moor. Beyond the highest point at Botton Head, the way drops gradually from Battersby Moor to Kildale.

Captain Cook's Monument and Roseberry Topping are both visited, before the National Park is left temporarily for the farmland route to the coast at Saltburn-on-Sea. Signs of industry (past and present) and high cliffs lead on to the picturesque fishing villages of Staithes and Runswick. Though outside the National Park, Whitby is a fascinating place, with its long harbour and bustling centre - one of the few sizeable towns actually on the Cleveland Way.

Hugging the sometimes unstable cliff edge, the way arrives at Robin Hood's Bay, another historic fishing village and popular tourist destination. Past Ravenscar and the tiny cove of Hayburn Wyke backed by delightful woods, Scarborough's conurbation is approached. Thereafter lies a short stretch to Filey Brigg where the Cleveland Way joins with the Wolds Way (to Hessle Haven, North Humberside), and the so-called 'Missing Link' back to Helmsley (see 'Missing Link).

Accommodation on or near the Cleveland Way is more plentiful in some areas than others, so planning is necessary, and in summer advance booking. A number of farms take lightweight tents, and there are Youth Hostels at Helmsley, Saltburn, Whitby, Boggle Hole and Scarborough. A list of accommodation is obtainable from the North York Moors National Park Information Service, The Old Vicarage, Bondgate, Helmsley, York.

START: Helmsley.
FINISH: Filey Brigg (or Helmsley via the 'Missing Link').
LENGTH: 93 miles (150km).
DETAILS: *A Guide to the Cleveland Way and Missing Link* by Malcolm Boyes (Constable). *The Cleveland Way* by Alan Falconer (HMSO). *Cleveland Way Companion* by Paul Hannon (Hillside)
OS MAPS: Sheets 93, 94, 99, 100 and 101.

A COAST TO COAST WALK (FINAL SECTION)

This fine long-distance trek from St. Bees in Cumbria to Robin Hood's Bay enters the North York Moors National Park at Ingleby Cross, near Osmotherley: though coincident with other routes at times, the crossing of the moors to the North Sea is a good walk in its own right - a very long day's hike indeed, or a less arduous 2 to 3 days' journey.

A climb up forest roads leads to Beacon Hill on Scarth Wood Moor and the start of the well-trod escarpment path switchbacking over Live Moor, Carlton Moor, Cringle and Cold Moors to Hasty Bank. Botton Head on Urra Moor is mounted (highest point on the North York Moors), and beyond Bloworth Crossing where the Cleveland Way veers sharply north, the Coast to Coast route takes to the track bed of the old Rosedale Ironstone Railway for some 5 miles (8km) round Farndale Head to the Lion Inn, Blakey, the first habitation since Huthwaite Green 16 miles back.

Fat Betty, a distinctive white cross at the head of Rosedale, precedes a boggy stretch round Great Fryup Head and a descent down the old Whitby road to Glaisdale. The valley of the River Esk forms a delightful contrast to the high moors as the route wends its way over Beggar's Bridge through East Arncliffe Wood to Egton Bridge and Grosmont, northern terminus of the North York Moors Railway.

A steep climb over heathery Sleights Moor takes walkers down to Littlebeck, a tiny hamlet nestling in a deep fold of the hills. Little Beck is followed upstream to Falling Foss waterfall, whereafter the way rises out over Sneaton Low Moor and Graystone Hills to Hawsker village. There ensues an exhilarating stretch of clifftop walking round Ness Point to the finish at Robin Hood's Bay.

START: St. Bees, Cumbria (final stage from Ingleby Cross).
FINISH: Robin Hood's Bay.
LENGTH: 190 miles (306km) - final stage 50 miles (80km).
DETAILS: *A Coast to Coast Walk* by A.Wainwright (Westmorland Gazette) - a pocket guide with maps and illustrations, widely available. The walk is also featured in:-
Classic Walks in Europe (Oxford Illustrated Press).
The National Trust Book of Long Walks by Adam Nicholson (Weidenfeld and Nicholson).
OS MAPS: 1″ Tourist Map - North York Moors.

THE CROSSES WALK *by Malcolm Boyes*

Starting and finishing at Goathland Village Hall, the North York Moors Crosses Walk links 13 of the best known ancient crosses on the moors. The route goes west to Botton Cross, Fat Betty (White Cross) and Ralph Crosses, south to Ana Cross, High Cross and Low Cross, north-east to Mauley Cross, Malo Cross and Lilla Cross. From Postgate Cross, the walk swings west back to Goathland via John Cross and York Cross.

The route was pioneered by Pete Gough, John Waind, Mick Horsley, Maurice and Malcolm Boyes and Colin Hood on the 2nd-3rd October 1971, with the assistance of Harry Benton and Betty Hood. It was given to the Scarborough and District Search and Rescue Team who have since organised the walk as an annual event (mid-July). All proceeds from the walk go towards the running costs of the rescue team. The event takes place on the first Saturday after the Lyke Wake Race and Osmotherley Gala.

START & FINISH: Goathland Village Hall.
LENGTH: 53 miles (85km).
DETAILS: *The Crosses Walk* by Malcolm Boyes (Dalesman Paperback). The event is an annual challenge, to be completed in 24 hours. For details. s.a.e. to Mrs. B.Hood, 21 St. Peters Street, Norton, Malton, North Yorkshire.
OS MAPS: Sheets 100, 101. Also recommended - 1:25,000 North York Moors, West and East sheets.

THE DERWENT WAY (FINAL SECTION)

As its title suggests, the Derwent Way shadows that river from its confluence with the Ouse to its source on the North York Moors. On paths, tracks and lanes close by the Derwent, the route crosses the Vale of York and skirts the Howardian Hills before reaching Malton. Now south of the river, the northern foothills of the Yorkshire Wolds are climbed and the river met again at West Ayton on the North York Moors National Park boundary.

The ensuing section of the way, which is relevant to this guide, is of excellent quality and worth walking even in its own right. The beautiful Forge Valley gives way to more open, pastoral country past Hackness Hall, then the riverside path threads secretively through Broxa Forest, emerging onto Harwood Dale Moor. The final leg over Burn Howe joins the Lyke Wake Walk path to Lilla Howe Cross, the oldest of all North York Moors Crosses and possibly Britain's oldest Christian monument.

START: Barmby-on-the-Marsh (final leg from West Ayton).
FINISH: Lilla Howe.
LENGTH: 90 miles (145km) total. Final leg approximately 14 miles (23km).
DETAILS: *The Derwent Way* by Richard C.Kenchington (Dalesman Books).
OS MAPS: Sheets 106, 105, 100 and 101.

THE ESKDALE WAY

The route taken by this circular walk crosses farmland, woods, dales, open moor and riverside pasture, sometimes on country lanes. Louis S.Dale, the originator, points out in his excellent booklet *Eskdale Way* that whilst an attempt has been made to take account of the need for overnight accommodation, this is in short supply in some areas, requiring a detour or extension to the day's stage. Moving from valley bottom to moor top on many occasions, a considerable amount of ascent and descent is involved, made worthwhile by the marvellous country traversed.

From the start at Whitby, a short section of clifftop walking precedes easterley progress inland through Ugglebarnby and over Sleights Moor to Grosmont. The Murk Esk is followed south towards Goathland, with a climb to Two Howes Rigg and Simon Howe leading to the Lyke Wake Walk path and the Roman Road on Wheeldale Moor.

A descent is made back north to Egton Bridge, whereafter the way mounts Glaisdale Head, over into Great Fryup Dale and up past 'Fat Betty' to Ralph Cross on Danby High Moor (the National Park logo). Beyond, the route drops into Westerdale and makes a loop round the remote Baysdale Moor to Baysdale Abbey and thence down to Kildale, the turning point of the walk.

Forestry plantations and moor lead north to Guisborough Woods

203

and back over to Commondale, the way now once more in the Esk Valley which is followed more closely to Castleton and Danby (where can be found the Moors Centre). Another climb attains Danby Beacon and a good track leads to the road and down to Lealholm.

Utilising more valley walking near railway and river, the way passes Glaisdale and Egton Bridge before diverting north of the river to Aislaby, thence via Ruswarp back to Whitby.

START & FINISH: Dock End, Whitby.
LENGTH: 82 miles (132km).
DETAILS: *Eskdale Way* by Louis S.Dale (Dalesman Books). An accommodation list is obtainable from the author: s.a.e. to Louis Dale, 10 Mulgrave View, Stainsacre, Whitby, North Yorkshire, YO22 4NX.
OS MAPS: Sheet 94.

THE ESK VALLEY WALK

The Esk Valley Walk comprises, in fact, 10 shorter ones joined together, and thus forms the basis for either a long hike of 30 miles, or a number of easier stages, broken up by taking overnight accommodation. It is eminently suitable for walkers of all abilities. Alternatively, sections of walking can be combined with progress by train to and from any British Rail station on the Esk Valley line, which for much of the route is close at hand.

The River Esk rises above Esklets at the head of remote Westerdale, to which the most straightforward access is along the track bed of the old Rosedale Ironstone Railway from the Lion Inn on Blakey Rigg between Farndale and Castleton. The infant Esk is followed down Westerdale in a pastoral landscape on paths, tracks and lanes to Castleton and Danby, home of the National Park Moors Centre.

A loop is made out of the valley to cross Beacon Hill and Brown Rigg End before the good moor track drops to Lealholm, after which river and railway are in close proximity through dales scenery. Glaisdale to Egton bridge takes walkers over Beggar's Bridge and on a paved pannier way through Arncliffe Wood, whereafter an old toll road leads to Grosmont and the northern terminus of the North York

Moors Historical Railway.

An old pannier way passes through woods and farmland along the valley, muddy in wet weather, and some road walking leads on to Ruswarp. Whitby is reached on footpaths and the Esk followed to its mouth at the harbour entrance.

START: Blakey bridge on Blakey Rigg - or the source of the Esk above Esklets in Westerdale.
FINISH: Whitby, west pier.
LENGTH: 30 miles (48km) - in total.
DETAILS: *The Esk Valley Walk* from the North York Moors National Park Information Service, The Old Vicarage, Bondgate, Helmsley, York (0439 70657). The walk is waymarked where necessary with a leaping salmon emblem (also standard footpath and bridleway waymarking).
OS MAPS: Sheet 94.

JOHN MERRILL'S NORTH YORK MOORS
CHALLENGE WALK *by John Merrill*

The North York Moors have always been a favourite walking area of mine, simply because of their scenic variety of moorland and coastal walking. The Cleveland Way was my first official long-distance walk, more than ten years ago. Since then I have walked it seven times as part of my training programme for my major walks.

Continuing my theme of Challenge Walks - others have been in the Peak District and Yorkshire Dales - I began looking at the North Yorkshire Moors. My aim has simply been to encompass the scenic variety found in the National Park - moorlands, valleys and coastal walking. At the same time, the walk is to be a challenge to complete within twelve hours, but within the capabilities of the average person. There is no time limit and the route does make a very enjoyable weekend walk of 24 miles, with 2000ft of ascent.

The route can be termed a 'seaside bash' or 'to the ocean and back'. There is a sting in the tail, for as you head for the ocean at Robin Hood's Bay, you are gradually descending, leaving the return to the moorland an ascent. I had several forays into the area trying out different paths and routes before I finally decided upon the route.

In early October, I set off from Goathland to piece the whole route together. As I would be note-taking on the way, and since the daylight hours were reduced, I planned a weekend circuit, with Robin Hood's

Bay as the overnight halt. I could not have chosen a better weekend. After weeks of rain the sun came out and enriched the glorious scene. I set off in a fibre pile jacket but soon stripped to T-shirt and shorts in the warm autumn weather. The views were extensive and, apart from a few walkers around May Beck, I had the countryside to myself. To me it was one of the most enjoyable weekend walks I had had for a long time.

I can only hope that on your walk you have equally as fine weather, and savour the variety of moorland and coastal walking. To me, the first sight of Whitby and later Robin Hood's Bay were magical moments, as I wove my way across the moorland and fields. Have a good walk and let me know how you fared.

Happy walking!

START & FINISH: Goathland.
LENGTH: 24 miles (39km).
DETAILS: *John Merrill's North Yorkshire Challenge Walk* booklet, available from J.N.M. Publications, Winster, Matlock, Derbyshire, DE4 2DQ. Four-colour embroidered badge, and certificate, available to the successful - apply to J.N.M. Publications.
OS MAP: Sheet 94.

THE LYKE WAKE WALK

Pioneered by Bill Cowley in 1955, the Lyke Wake Walk is perhaps the best known and most frequently walked route over the North York Moors. It starts near Osmotherley, follows the undulating northern escarpment over Live Moor, Carlton Bank, Cringle Moor and Hasty Bank to reach Botton Head on Urra Moor before crossing the main North York Moors watershed east over Farndale, Rosedale, Wheeldale and Goathland Moors. Beyond the North York Moors Railway in Newtondale, Fylingdales early-warning station's 'golf-balls' dominate the landscape: from Lilla Howe, the route gradually descends to Beacon Howes and the Raven Hall Hotel, Ravenscar, right on the cliff edge. To qualify for membership of the Lyke Wake Club, the 40-mile (64km) crossing must be completed within 24 hours (14 to 18 hours is the summer average).

When Bill Cowley and his companions first walked the route back in 1955, much of it was undefined across heather moor (it is still thus marked on the OS 1″ Tourist Map). However, hundreds of thousands of pairs of feet have tramped the same way since, and not only has a path developed, but in many places (especially in the central peaty sections and where it is coincident with other routes), it has become badly eroded. *SPECIAL NOTE: The National Park is asking for parties to be kept small and for large sponsored walks to go elsewhere (see the 'Shepherds' Round' as an alternative).*

Because of its popularity with large groups of walkers and support parties (10,000 crossings have been recorded in one year alone!), trouble has arisen in the past over night-time disturbances to local residents, litter and vehicle parking. For practical purposes, the walk now starts from the car park at the east end of Cod Beck reservoir, the first past the cattle grid from Osmotherley. Please be sure to show maximum consideration for other people. (eg. in cafés and hotels) and for the environment itself. Parts of the walk are on concessionary footpaths across private land, agreed with landowners and tenants: straying off them is to be avoided if at all possible. In any event, cycling or horse-riding are permitted on only a few stretches, and it is illegal to take any motor-vehicle more than 15m off the road.

Finally, the Lyke Wake Walk can be anything from an exhilarating summer romp to a grim battle with the elements: winter crossings are not generally recommended. It is essential to be properly equipped for a serious upland expedition, to have a walk plan and inform others of it, to obtain a weather forecast before setting off and to be fit enough not to endanger your own safety or that of others.

START: Sheepwash car park, Scarth Wood Moor, near Osmotherley, (traditionally the OS trig. point on Beacon Hill).
FINISH: Beacon Howes, Ravenscar.
LENGTH: 40 miles (64km).
DETAILS: *The Lyke Walk Walk and the Lyke Wake Way* by Bill Cowley (Dalesman Books) - £3 inc. postage. A few copies of *Lyke Wake Walk* by Bill Cowley (the original book) are still left - £2 inc. postage. Both from bookshops or the Lyke Wake Club, Goulton Grange, Swainby, Northallerton, Yorks.

Successful crossings are rewarded by various orders of membership, such as 'Dirgers' and 'Witches', according to the number of crossings achieved. Send 20p and s.a.e. for each crossing reported, to receive a Condolence Card and entry in the records. Reports on the walk may be pungent or poetic - quotable ones are welcome - but keep purely factual ones brief. S.a.e. to the Lyke Wake Club (address above) for list of various publications, events and badges etc. available.

A free leaflet on Moorland Safety is available from National Park Information Centres, or s.a.e. to North York Moors National Park, Bondgate, Helmsley, York YO6 5BP. (0439) 70657.

OS MAPS: Sheets 99, 93, 94. Or 1″ Tourist Map of North York Moors.

THE 'MISSING LINK' *by Malcolm Boyes*

This 50 mile (80km) route from the coast near Burniston, north of Scarborough, crosses the moors and forests to Helmsley, turning the Cleveland Way into a circuit. The route was first walked by June and Peter Gough, Colin Hood and Maurice and Malcolm Boyes in May 1975.

The route passes through Broxa Forest and along the ridge of Cross-cliffe to Saltergate. It then passes the Hole of Horcum to Levisham and Stape, through Cropton Forest to Lastingham and Hutton-le-Hole, the final section being through Farndale and around Birk Nab to descend Riccaldale to Helmsley. The walk is usually undertaken in two or three days, with stops at Lockton youth hostel or Levisham and around Hutton-le-Hole.

START: Crook Ness, north of Scarborough.
FINISH: Helmsley.
LENGTH: 50 miles (80km).
DETAILS: *The Cleveland Way and Missing Link* by Malcom Boyes (Constable) - now out of print, but another guide likely to replace it.
OS MAPS: Sheets 100, 101.

REASTY TO ALLERSTON FOREST WALK

This route takes walkers through 16 miles (26km) of upland forest, from Reasty Bank (near Silpho) south to Allerston on the A170 near Thornton Dale. Throughout the walk, directions are waymarked using a 'Blue Man' symbol, and on completion the walker may purchase a special 'Blue Man' badge.

START: Reasty Bank car park.
FINISH: Allerston.
LENGTH: 16 miles (26km).
DETAILS: For an A4 sheet giving a list of grid references for the
route, send s.a.e. or visit the Dalby Forest Visitor Centre, Forestry
Commission, Low Dalby, Pickering, Yorks, YO18 7LT. Also
available from the same address are 'Blue Man' badges and details of
other walks and recreational facilities in the local forests.
OS MAP: Sheet 101.

THE NEWTONDALE TRAIL

A 'must' for steam railway enthusiasts who are also keen walkers, this
route follows the course of the North York Moors Railway through
Newtondale, from its southern terminus at Pickering to its northern
one at Grosmont.

Some sections of the trail are close by the railway, others use tracks
through forest and over open moors high above Newtondale which
forms the 'spine' of this walk. The trail is by no means an arduous
one, though longer than a mere stroll. Successful completion is
awarded by a badge.

START: Pickering.
FINISH: Grosmont.
LENGTH: 20 miles (32km).
DETAILS: Free A4 outline route sheet, to be used in conjunction
with an OS map, along with badge details - s.a.e. to Mike Teanby,
Lyndhurst, Sutton Road, Thirsk, North Yorks.
OS MAPS: Sheets 100, 94.

THE SAMARITAN WAY

Originated by Teesdale Samaritans as a fund-raising venture, the
Samaritan Way uses several already established routes to make a tough
40 mile (64km) circuit of the high moors to the south of Guisborough.

From Guisborough, the route leads south over Commondale, across
Great Fryup Dale, Glaisdale and Farndale Moors, returning via
Westerdale and Baysdale. The Cleveland Way is followed from

Captain Cook's Monument to High Cliff Nab above Guisborough.

START & FINISH: Guisborough.
LENGTH: 40 miles (64km).
DETAILS: There are 2 classes of badge and certificate available for
successful walkers. For free outline route sheet and badge/certificate
details, send s.a.e. to Richard Pinkney, 11 Pine Road, Ormsby,
Middlesborough, Cleveland.
OS MAPS: Sheets 94, 100 and 93.

THE SEAHORSE SAUNTER *by Stephen Watkins*

SEAHORSE
SAUNTER

Stride on, and we will turn our back
On Yorkshire's Vale below;
We'll cross the mighty uplands,
That oft times are blown with snow.

Stride on, across the sweet land,
Through forests, over gills;
We'll climb out of the valley
Over lush, green Hambleton Hills.

Stride on past ancient coal pits,
Past iron workings too,
Cross old, forlorn railway lines
Where long past steam trains drew.

Stride on and cross the purple ling,
Along the pannierman's way;
Perhaps you'll hear the bell horse ring
On the leading Cleveland Bay.

Stride on, into the green dale
And Cross the Beggar's Bridge,
Pass through ancient woodlands
To the open moorland ridge.

Stride on, down the toll road,
Along Esk Dale's valley floor;
Ignore the wain carts charges,
For they apply no more.

Stride on and hear the mournful toll
That warns of Cleveland Roak;

We've many miles yet still to tread
To see the Whitby boat.

Stride on, to stand o'er Whitby Town
Where, two centuries ago,
Without a guide to cross the moors,
A stranger dared not go.

Although devised as a backpacking weekend, the route of the Seahorse Saunter was soon seen as a possible alternative to the troubled Lyke Wake Walk and its erosion problems. Consequently, the Saunter held its inaugural walk in May of 1984, to record a time of 14 hours 55 mins.

In due course, the enthusiastic reaction of groups led by the author prompted the publication of a guide sheet. Since then, the walk has gained in popularity, with almost equal numbers of single day crossings and leisurely weekends being recorded. Whether you choose to challenge the current fastest time of 9 hours 30 mins. (West Yorkshire L.D.W.A.), or saunter the route over two or more days, the route offers both variety and interest.

Starting from the White Horse of Kilburn, the walk follows field paths, bridleways and paved packhorse paths to make a north-easterly crossing of the North York Moors National Park, to reach Whitby on the east coast.

Along its 43 mile (69km) length, the route attains nearly 6000ft (1829m) of ascent as it climbs in and out of the steep-sided glaciated dales that penetrate the moors. The rich foliage in the first 12 miles (19km) suddenly gives way to a purple hue as the traditional moors are encountered. Once past half way, the open expanse of moorland gradually subsides to the more enclosed greenery of the Esk Valley. Upon cresting the penultimate rise, the ruined Abbey will make a fitting backdrop to the historic rooftops of Old Whitby as the town unfurls below. The 'sting in the tail' to the walk is the arduous climb up to the top of the famous 199 steps, and so to the end of the walk.

START: The Kilburn White Horse.
FINISH: The 199 steps at Whitby.
LENGTH: 43 miles (69km).
DETAILS: For full route description, along with details of badges, accommodation, etc. send a s.a.e. to Stephen Watkins (Recorder), 36 Barons Crescent, St. Giles Park, Copmanthorpe, York, YO2 3TZ.

(Badges available for all finishers, but certificate only to those completing the route within 24 hours.)
OS MAPS: Sheets 100 and 94.

THE SHEPHERDS' ROUND

This walk, a tough circuit of the North York Moors involving 5000ft (1524m) of ascent, has been designed as an alternative to the Lyke Wake Walk whose path has suffered serious erosion in places from the volume of walkers on the route, especially large groups. The Shepherds' Round is over ancient definitive footpaths and bridleways on generally firmer terrain and has the added advantage of being a circular route, starting and finishing from Sheepwash car park, near Osmotherley (the same start as for the Lyke Wake Walk).

A 3-colour woven cloth badge is available for completion within 24 hours, but the circuit makes an excellent 2-day walk with overnight accommodation at Fangdale Beck/Hawnby. Large groups of walkers and support parties are asked to show consideration for local residents (especially at night-time), not to leave litter, to park vehicles thoughtfully and to respect the natural habitats through which the walk passes. Being the same length and over similar terrain as the Lyke Wake Walk, the Shepherds' Round is no easier option. It is important to be properly equipped, to inform others of your walk plan, to obtain a weather forecast and to be fit enough to ensure your own safety and that of others.

The route itself follows a well-trodden path along the northern escarpment of the Cleveland Hills, in common with several other routes, including the Lyke Wake Walk, Cleveland Way and Coast to Coast Walk. Urra Moor is traversed to Blowath Crossing, here turning south down Rudland Rigg to Cockayne in the remote head of Bransdale. Up on the moortops again, the route threads over to Bilsdale near Fangdale Beck. Heading west, it runs down Wether House Beck to Honey Hill ruin, whence a good track leads south-west

212

and onto the public road into Hawnby. A rough lane climbs to the old Hambleton Drove Road which is taken north over Black Hambleton and, with a short stretch of road walking, back to the Sheepwash car park.

START & FINISH: Sheepwash car park, Scarth Wood Moor, near Osmotherley.
LENGTH: 40 miles (64km).
DETAILS: S.a.e. and 25p to Lyke Wake Club, Goulton Grange, Swainby, Northallerton, Yorks. for a route leaflet, accommodation and badge list. A brief report of your circuit, with any useful comments, is also welcome. (Badges only for circuits completed within 24 hours - allow at least 18 hours average).
OS MAPS: Sheets 100, 93, 94.
　　　　Or 1″ Tourist Map of North York Moors.

THE WHITE ROSE WALK *by George Garbutt*

Linking two well-known landmarks, the Kilburn White Horse and Roseberry Topping, much of the White Rose Walk follows the western escarpment of the Hambleton and Cleveland Hills. The total heights climbed on the long and medium variants is about 4900ft (1493m), and on the short variant 3700ft (1128m). Walkers in good condition should complete the crossing within the hours of daylight during the summer and the walk falls within the area covered by the North York Moors Tourist map.

The Yorkshire Wayfarers Rambling Club decided in 1968 that it was time for a change to the existing west-east or east-west crossings of the North York Moors. A north-south route was thought of and, because the western escarpment offers some of the more dramatic views, members and friends spent time in 1967 exploring the area and linking up favourite walks and strolls. The grandeur of the Hambleton and Cleveland cliffs, the romance of the Drove Road, the long stretches of green track over heather moors and the dramtic land forms at start and finish, all had their influence in the selection of the

213

route.

Naming of the walk was almost automatic, linking the 'white' of the Kilburn White Horse with the 'rose' of Roseberry Topping in the county of the White Rose. The walk was completed for the first time by the Wayfarers on 1st June 1968.

START: South of Newton-under-Roseberry.
FINISH: Kilburn White Horse.
LENGTH: Long route 37 miles (60km); medium route 34 miles (55km); short route 31 miles (50km).
DETAILS: *The White Rose Walk* by Geoffrey White (Dalesman Books). Successful White Rose walkers may apply for a Congratulations Card (20p each), rucksack badge (80p), pin badge (£1), tie, bearing a single badge emblem on blue, green or maroon backgrounds (£3.75p). Book, items and list - s.a.e. to George Garbutt, White Rose Walk Recorder, 17 Kingsclere, Huntington, York, YO3 9SF.
OS MAPS: Sheets 93, 94. Or 1″ Tourist Map of North York Moors.

Stone Causeway (see p.51)

APPENDIX 1: History and the Moors

In 1821, caves were unearthed in the walls of a quarry in Kirkdale, on the Park's southern edge. They were found to contain the bones and teeth of many animal species, including mammoth, rhinoceros, hyena and lion, and represent the oldest archaeological material discovered in the National Park.

After the Great Ice Age, big fluctuations in climate, vegetation and tree-cover profoundly affected early man's ability to settle the area. Until around 8000BC, it was virtually devoid of human life altogether, after which time nomadic hunters from the Mesolithic Age periodically wandered over the moors, leaving behind them a few 'pygmy flints'. The climate then was cool and dry enough for hunting on the high moortops, augmented by river fishing.

Oval mounds up to 165ft (50m) long, made of stones and gravel, are Neolithic long barrows, the burial places of New Stone Age man dating back to 2000BC. Typical examples are found at Kepwick, Ayton East Field and Scamridge.

It was the incursion of 'Beaker Folk' from the continent around 1800BC, however, that heralded the Bronze Age and led to the development of food vessel pottery, numerous specimens of which can be seen in Whitby and Scarborough museums. The climate was becoming warmer and encouraged the spread of woodlands containing oak, ash, lime and alder. Following a previous wetter 'Atlantic' period, the moors were once again dry. Pastures and grazing were good and grain could be cultivated successfully - it was perhaps the most favourable time of all for an occupation of the land and Bronze Age man flourished, leaving many remains. Large tumuli, frequent groupings of small cairns, and stone circles are among the more evident Bronze Age relics. There are few traces of pastoral farming, probably because permanent shelters were unnecessary in the equable climate; huntsmen, however, did leave many flint arrowheads.

Several modest stone circles still exist, their components dispersed down the centuries for use as gateposts, and in any case nothing to compare with a Stonehenge or an Avebury. Sites include High Bride Stones (5 miles, 8km, south-west of Whitby), Standing Stones Rigg (6 miles, 9.5km, north-west of Scarborough), Blakey Topping (7 miles, 11km, north-east of Pickering), Bride Stones (Bilsdale East Moor), Danby Rigg, and Flat Howe on Sleights Moor.

Circular stone barrows on ridges and moor tops are thought to have been the burial places of more important Bronze Age people. Larger

215

Kirkdale Caves

Bronze-Age 'howe' near Goathland

ones carry the name 'howe' (from the Scandinavian *haugr* for buriaı mound), as in Lilla Howe and Green Howe - their conspicuous humps punctuating the long moorland horizon. Loose and Western Howes on Danby High Moor presented modern historians with much valuable material, including skin clothing, human remains, dugout canoes, a battle-axe and bronze dagger. Over the passage of time, however, many barrows have been ransacked and their contents lost for ever, much of it sold to private collectors by Victorian plunderers who, of course, kept no records of their booty.

Iron Age man had to contend with a climate both colder and wetter than ours today. The moors would have been bleak, boggy places indeed and it comes as no surprise to find fields and settlements sited on the lower slopes in sheltered locations, and reaching no further north than Castle Hill, Scarborough. A few earthwork promontory forts dating from around 2000BC can be found, notably those at Boltby Scar in the Hambleton Hills and at Roulston Scar on Sutton Bank.

Dykes are a fairly common feature on the moors, some extending up to a mile in length. Good examples are Cleave Dyke, crossing the head of Sutton Bank, the Urra Moor Dykes, Park Dyke on the western

Wade's Causeway, Wheeldale Moor

escarpment, and Scamridge Dykes 3 miles (5km) north of Ebberston. The dykes are hard to date with any certainty and may be medieval in origin.

There are relatively few Roman remains, though Wade's Causeway - running north-east from Cawthorn Camp towards the River Esk and the coast north of Whitby - is one of the best preserved ways of its kind in Britain. It marches across Pickering and Wheeldale Moors but is at its most impressive near Hunt House, south-west of Goathland, where excavations have revealed its remarkable raised foundations of flat stones on gravel, provided with lateral drains.

Cawthorn Camp, on a ridge between Newtondale and Rosedale, was used by the Romans as a military training area for garrisons from York around 110-120AD. Today there is not a great deal to see: four over-grown enclosures of earth mounds, turf ramparts and ditches.

Against attacks from Saxon pirates and Scottish Picts, the Romans erected a series of signal stations along the coast, though they may only have been in use for some 20 years. Each took the form of a high lookout tower behind a protective wall and ditch. Scarborough's Castle Hill remains are well worth seeing, as are those at Huntcliffe (1 mile 2km, east of Saltburn), Goldsborough, Ravenscar and Filey.

The Romans left Britain in 410AD and a northward migration by Angles took place, using Roman roads and the coast. Pagan remains from the 6th century have been found at Saltburn and Robin Hood's Bay, suggesting the existence of clifftop villages. There was still no widespread permanent settlement of the north-eastern hills by the 7th century, though the Angles now occupied south-facing foothills. Their place-names often ended in '-ley' or '-ton', hence Pockley, Appleton, Ebberston, etc. and the considerable number of such names indicates successful farming on hillsides or in woodland clearings near good pasture.

9th century Danish invaders soon accepted Christianity: 'kirkby' was their name for 'church-town' and '-by' for a small farm or hamlet, especially on the western edge of the moors, hence Battersby, Ingleby, Swainby, etc. The Danes also erected carved stone crosses at church sites which were often incorporated later into stone churches, built to replace the timber structures of the Norse period. There are 10th century Anglo-Danish crosses at Arncliff, Oswaldkirk and Kirkbymoorside. Anglo-Norse crosses are much more common, as for example at Hawsker, Levisham, Lastingham, Upleatham and Ellerburn.

Stone crosses encountered today by travellers on the central moorlands were possibly put there by the monasteries as navigational landmarks and to provide reassuring spiritual guidance, though a lack of hard evidence leaves them surrounded by mystery and enigma. Several are very well known - Lilla Cross (the oldest Christian monument in N. England), Fat Betty and Stump Cross to name but three - and most appear on O.S. maps. Young Ralph Cross on Rosedale Head has been adopted as the North York Moors National Park logo.

The moors supported Norse sheep farmers while valleys and foothills became progressively more settled. By 1086, when the Domesday census was made, 69 communities within the present National Park region were deemed worthy of mention. In the 12th century, Cistercian monks found the more remote, unpopulated areas of North Yorkshire ideal for their retreats and spiritual centres. Great abbeys such as Rievaulx and Byland were established, adding a significant contribution to sheep farming on the poorer uplands.

Quarries became widespread as the demand for stone to build houses, barns, sheepfolds, religious edifices and castles increased. The latter, as well as defending against raids by Scots from across the border, also helped control a still scattered population, with hamlets and villages centred on clearings in the great Royal Forest. Castles at

St. Gregory's Minster, a pre-conquest church in Kirkdale

Helmsley Scar and Pickering are fine examples, as is that at Danby, wherein Henry VIII's sixth wife, Catherine Parr, lived for a while.

Whitby and Scarborough were great medieval ports and Captain Cook, whose navigational skills led to adventure and discovery in the South Pacific, is a local celebrity of national renown. A strong sea-faring tradition exists along the coast and most communities have experienced their share of tragedy in the face of an often hostile North Sea.

Herring fishing once thrived, but for the most part people looked inland to the hills and dales rather than to the sea for their livelihoods. The alum and ironstone industries brought new vitality and an influx of labour to the area during the last century but the bonanza lasted little longer than a generation. George Stephenson brought the railway to Whitby through Newtondale and opened up Scarborough and Bridlington to mill-workers starved of fresh air and sunshine. The line still lives, operating as the privately-run North York Moors Railway from Pickering to Grosmont, where it connects with British Rail's Middlesborough to Whitby service.

In order to shift commodities to and from market and coast, an intricate web of tracks, paths and packhorse ways evolved over the centuries: a debt is surely owed by the present walking fraternity to our forbears for establishing such a comprehensive network of routes over all kinds of terrain.

Since the arrival of the motor car in these parts during the 1930's, some ancient tracks and byways have been overlaid with tarmac, ensuring speedy communication between settlements and greatly reducing their isolation. Many of the old ways remain either wholly or partially intact, however, leading the present-day walker from dale to moor top and often past sites of great antiquity. At such places, a considerable leap of imagination is needed to span the immense technological and cultural gap between ourselves and those ancestors whose ancient marks so intrigue us.

Ralph Cross, the National Park emblem

APPENDIX 2:   Notes on Geology within the Park

The North York Moors National Park is a uniquely interesting geological region of Yorkshire, defined by clear physical boundaries: to the north, Tees-side and the Middlesborough conurbation, to the west the Vale of Mowbray, to the south the Vale of York and to the east the North Sea. Rock types and structures, fossil remains, evidence of glacial history and continuing erosion by frost, wind, rain and waves are all there for the observant visitor - particularly to the walker, whose view of the landscape is always an intimate one.

Around 150 million years ago in the Jurassic Period, muds and silts were laid down which, under geological pressure, were to form the sedimentary rocks characterising the North York Moors. In fact, these rocks are thought to have originated near the equator, moving to their present position on the plates which make up the earth's crust.

Sandstones and ironstones of the Lias group of rocks have been extensively exploited by man, especially in the vicinity of Staithes and the Murk Esk valley. Elsewhere, grey shales and limestones contain numerous fossils, exposed well on eroded coastal stretches between Redcar and Ravenscar. Further inland, the harder sandstone cap has been cut through by streams, allowing the excavation of valleys such as Eskdale, Rosedale and Farndale in the soft Lias shales.

The same sandstone used widely as a building material occurs as crags and outcrops, particularly in the Park's northern section where they are used by climbers. Along with the shales of the high moors, these rocks - known as the Ravenscar group - were originally deposited as sand and mud in a vast river delta which was repeatedly inundated by the sea: they bear many examples of fossilised plant and animal life.

During the final marine invasion, particles of lime attached to tiny grains of sand and shell (called 'ooliths') became cemented together and constitute another group of rocks known as the Middle Oolitic. Today they form the Tabular and Hambleton Hills from Scarborough to Helmsley, including the south-west escarpment. Kimmeridge clays, best known on the Dorset coast after which place they are named, underlie the Vale of Pickering, though more recent deposits obscure their identification.

The sedimentary rocks of the high moors themselves are all-encompassing, except for a narrow intrusion of igneous rock - a lava flow from 58 million years ago. This is called the Cleveland Dyke or Whinstone Ridge and runs roughly north-west to south-east across the Park. It was quarried and crushed extensively for road building during the first half of this century.

What we now know as north-east Yorkshire has been elevated from sea and river bed to dry land during the past 70 million years. It has been a gentle uplifting, with no titanic convulsions of the earth's crust to impose dramatic folding. Faults and breaks in the strata occur mainly on the coast, where erosion is at its fiercest and some 2 inches (5cm) per year are lost to the sea.

The North York Moors sedimentary rocks yield many signs of their ancient origins and are famous for the abundance and variety of fossils. Ammonites are especially numerous, their flat, coiled shells

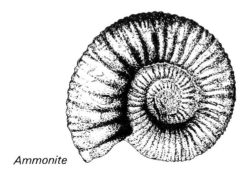

Ammonite

Low-tide 'scars' of Lias Limestone near Staithes

occasionally reaching 2ft (60cm) in diameter and assuming considerable variations in form and pattern. Whitby has incorporated three ammonites into the design of its town crest, testimony to their relatively widespread occurence.

During th 18th and 19th centuries, an increase in scientific curiosity about our geological past, aided by quarrying activity which exposed hitherto unseen strata, led to the unearthing of numerous fossilised reptiles, including the impressions of dinosaurs' curious 3-toed footsteps in the Lias shales of this part of Yorkshire: specimens are spread far and wide in museums across Britain.

During the Great Ice Age, the North York Moors - then desolate snowfields and tundra - would have been surrounded on three sides by ice many hundreds of feet thick. Evidence is clear today in the sands and gravels left by the melting ice, the glacial boulder clays and the meltwater channels subsequently left dry (such as Forge Valley and Newtondale Gorge), or running contary to natural drainage.

Sea-cut, the original pre-Ice-Age course of the River Derwent

Sticky brown clay along the coast - debris from a retreating glacier - holds interesting clues as to the nature and movement of that ice cover, for in it have been found 'erratic' boulders carried here from Scotland, the Lake District and as far afield as Scandinavia. The ice-sheet was to advance and retreat several times before warmer conditions became established around 10,000 years ago, a mere blinking of the eye in geological time.

APPENDIX 3: Mining and Quarrying

Elaborate necklaces made from jet have been found in Bronze Age burial mounds: the appeal of this fossilised conifer which is easy to carve and polish has a long history. Although greatly admired and used by the Romans, the zenith of its exploitation in Yorkshire was reached in the 1870's. The industry was centred on Whitby, where over 1500 people were employed making jet ornaments in 200 dusty workshops. Hard jet was valued more highly than the soft variety, and carvers often specialised in subjects, such as heads or fruit and foliage. Changing fashions and the importation of cheap Spanish jet led to the industry's decline by the turn of this century but it always was, in any case, rather a speculative occupation, the jet pieces being scattered randomly in the shale beds and not easy to extract. It is still worked on a small scale - raw jet often collected from seashore locations and no longer mined in quantity, as it once was from cliffs and dales alike.

Prodigious amount of alum were quarried from the Cleveland Hills and the coast between the 17th and mid-19th centuries. It was used in the dyeing and tanning industries until a cheaper alternative was discovered in colliery waste. Today, the slag heaps of pink shale waste and the scar of huge terraced quarries are still visible in places such as Boulby and Loftus, Saltwick Nab, Sandsend and near Ravenscar.

The presence of a suitable supply of sand and timber encouraged glass-makers from France to settle near the southern end of Rosedale in the 16th century. Remains of their main furnace, uncovered at the site in 1968/69, has been reconstructed in the Ryedale Folk Museum at Hutton-le-Hole, though its exact original dimensions have not been established with total certainty.

The Jurassic rocks of these north-eastern moors were exploited, above all, for their iron-ore. Amongst other locations, Rievaulx Abbey had a forge in operation by the mid-16th century and other workings date back to medieval times. Oak charcoal was the prime fuel for furnaces then, and it is thought that the depletion of natural woodland, along with transportation difficulties, caused the demise of this early phase of the industry.

By 1800, ironstone was being collected from shoreline deposits at Saltburn and Scarborough by the Tyne Iron Company. Not until 1836, however, were mining operations begun in a seam at Grosmont, leading to the coast at Skinningrove. Subsequently, further ore fields were found around Guisborough and along the northern slopes of the Cleveland Hills.

In 1856, the modern working of ironstone in and around Rosedale

Ironstone kilns at Rosedale East Mines

began, following the discovery of an unusually thick, metal-rich vein in the dale side a mile south of Rosedale Abbey. Ore was taken out in horse-drawn wagons to Pickering along a road described at the time as 'a complete bog from end to end; full of clay holes 2 feet deep' - and thence by rail to various ironworks.

When the North Eastern Railway came to Rosedale in 1861, ore was rope-hauled up an incline tramway and along Spaunton Moor to large kilns. Here, carbonic acid gas and water were 'roasted' off, reducing the weight of ironstone to be transported out. This process, known as 'calcination', yielded large quantities of calcine dust, rich in iron oxide - a resource in its own right which was removed for industrial processing in nearby Tees-side after about 1920.

More mines were opened in the area, some using horizontal 'drifts', others vertical shafts. Coal mines were sunk to supply railway engines and steam-driven winches. On the moors and dale sides there sprung up an infrastructure of railway tracks, kilns, hoppers, chimneys, rows of cottages and other associated buildings. By the early 1870's, industrial activity was at its height and a single-track, standard gauge line was in use between Battersby, near Great Ayton, and West Rosedale Bank Top, a distance of 14 miles (22.5km); a spur was added round Rosedale Head to the East Mines complex. From Battersby, the line reached the foot of the northern Cleveland escarpment and wagons were hauled by cable up Ingleby Incline to 1370ft (418m) on Greenhow Moor. Trains then operated between here and the mines on a track which wound cunningly round the heads of Bransdale and Farndale without recourse to bridge or tunnel.

The sheer audacity of the Rosedale Ironstone Railway bears witness to the vigour of the ironstone industry at that time. Conditions on or near the moor tops were often severe yet men from local villages walked to and from the workings on rough moorland tracks in all weathers. Snow sometimes completely blocked the railway and brought mining operations to a standstill, while gales were a regular hazard.

After 1920, the higher quality of imported ore, combined with the effects of the General Strike in 1926, sounded the industry's death knell: with 65 years of operation behind it, the Rosedale railway finally closed on 13th June 1929. What remains today of the mine buildings, terracing, cottages and spoil heaps, and especially the old railway track bed, are fascinating reminders of a recent chapter in our industrial history.

There is much to see. Although not a public right-of-way throughout its whole length, the railway track is walked by many, both as part of long-distance trails over the moors such as the Coast to Coast Walk and Lyke Wake Walk, and for its own sake as a unique evocation of an era gone forever. An excellent booklet all about the Rosedale mines and railway, illustrated with old photographs, is published by Scarborough Archaeological and Historical Society (Research Report No.9).

Many overgrown and neglected quarries within the National Park once yeilded sandstone, a ubiquitous building material much in demand for mining and railway structures around the turn of the century. Though put to mostly local use, quarries near Whitby furnished the stone for Covent Garden Market, Waterloo Bridge and the Houses of Parliament. Limestone is currently in favour for new domestic building, and important workings exist in the south of the Park near Helmsley and Appleton-le-Moors; at Pickering, the stone is crushed for agricultural use.

The North York Moors are underpinned by deep rocks from the Permian Age, formed 200 million years ago during desert conditions.

Boulby Potash Mine

The potash they contain is useful in agriculture and is being profitably extracted near Whitby and at Boulby, though not without some scenic and environmental sacrifices having been made.

APPENDIX 4: Flora and Fauna
(a) The Moors

Great forests of birch and pine once covered the moors. Although some species such as rowan and sessile oak still survive in sheltered spots, the tree cover has long since disappeared beneath the combined onslaught of a changing climate, man's prodigious appetite for timber, and foraging by pigs, cattle and goats which had already decimated the woodlands by the end of the Middle Ages.

Today, much of the moorland is clothed in heather and ling - the largest continuous expanse in England and occupying 40% of the National Park area. Though often dry, with sandstone outcrops, conditions can be wet and boggy too, but in late summer these high landscapes are lit up by a glorious purple haze as heather and ling come into flower.

Each summer, over 6,000 beehives are installed on the moors, each hive containing upwards of 40,000 bees. Their industrious search for nectar creates a persistent background hum, and in a good year as much as 120,000 jars of rich, dark honey is produced.

Without careful management, the heather would deteriorate and no longer support its population of sheep and grouse. Because only 15% of each year's new growth is grazed, vast areas of heather would rapidly become too high for sheep to move about freely in, tough woody stems of no value as grazing. Both sheep and grouse eat the tender young shoots which are encouraged by periodic burning-back of the mature plants. This is carried out between 1st November and 31st March each winter, the burned-off areas known locally as 'swiddens'. At the same time, grouse need some denser heather as cover, so the moors often resemble a patchwork of varying levels of vegetation.

In dry weather, fire is a serious danger to moorland plants, which may take many years to regenerate: as often as not they succumb to colonisation by bracken. Despite relieving the moors' sombre colours with a dash of springtime green, bracken has spread widely during the past half-century in the rough pasture above intake walls and here and there over the tops - an unwelcome invasion. Bilberry, crowberry, bell heather and cotton grass are also common, with cowberry found at the head of some smaller dales.

Rarer plants occur in a few localities, principally in the Saltergate and Goathland areas, while the 4 square miles of Fylingdales Moors closed to the public contain flora which may otherwise have suffered from the attentions (not always considerate) of visitors. In general,

Grouse-shooting butt

plants flower earlier on the sunnier south and west slopes of the moors than on those exposed to the north and east.

Red grouse share the moorland habitat with other resident and visiting species, but unlike them are shot in the name of 'sport' for 4 months each autumn: shooting butts are common on all the central moors. Other moorland birds likely to be seen by the walker include curlew, golden plover and lapwing, as well as kestrel, the occasional harrier and the much rarer merlin, with its low, rapid flight. Bracken on or near the tops is often frequented by meadow pipit, skylark, wheatear, whinchat, carrion crow and pheasant. Good seasons for observation are spring and early summer which trigger a crescendo of bird activity.

Adders and slow worms may be encountered on moor and in dale alike, as may the signs of fox and badger, while common lizards are partial to sunning themselves on dry stone walls. The limited range of flora on the moors supports a modest number of insect species which include the northern eggar moth and typical butterflies such as the common heath and green hairstreak.

(b) The Dales

Life in the sheltered dales is far kinder than on adjacent moorland and a corresponding proliferation of wildlife can be expected. Many exquisite wild flowers, too numerous to list, thrive in the dales of the

Above Little Beck

limestone belt, nestling beneath mixed woodland of ash, birch, wych elm and sessile oak, especially in the unfelled valleys. Herbs are found here too, some rare and beautiful species in evidence.

The marsh orchid and other uncommon plants growing in the wet meadows of the limestone belt are threatened by ploughing and drainage schemes, which radically alter the character of such fragile habitats. In contrast, dry grasslands support thistles and rock rose amongst other species, while fly and bee orchids and deadly night-shade may be found in the many disused quarries.

Of the non-limestone dales, Farndale has long been one of the most popular, once known as the 'Dale of Daffodils'. Increased access-ibility with the advent of the motor car led to over-picking, trampling and even commercial exploitation of the flowers and for a time their very existence was endangered. Farndale, however, is now a designated Nature Reserve and its daffodils, along with those in other southern dales, are protected for everyone to enjoy.

Bluebells, violets and wood anemones are abundant throughout the dales, as is lady's mantle, while rosebay adds vibrant colour to recently felled woodland. Drooping sedge and giant horsetail are common in Forge Valley, Riccal Dale and in small coastal valleys.

For the most part, the dales are cultivated land, with arable crops on higher stretches, and valley floors often down to grass. Regrettably, many original plants have disappeared in the move to new grass mixtures.

A significant 18% of the National Park is occupied by the Forestry Commission's North Yorkshire Forest - substantial plantations of fast growing pine, larch and spruce. Although deer roam in parts of Dalby and Allerston forests, the communial huddle of trees generally excludes light and life, creating an eery gloom totally devoid of greenery. Happily for the walker, numerous forest tracks and rides provide easy access, as well as giving welcome shelter in rough weather.

The rivers Rye, Esk and Derwent are popular with anglers. Trout are present in most streams, though frequently below takeable size in the upper reaches. Grayling are plentiful in the Rye and Derwent, and

Grayling

salmon run up the Esk. Smaller species such as crayfish, minnow and brook lamprey occur in the Upper Derwent, while eels are present in nearly all rivers, lakes and ponds. (NOTE: Fishing in rivers and reservoirs is by permit only.)

Stretches of water such as Gormire Lake (the Park's only natural lake), Scaling Dam and Boltby Reservoir are favourite haunts for botanists and bird-watchers: over 130 bird species alone were recorded in a recent survey. The large number of bird species nesting in and visiting the dales are well represented in Forge Valley, 3 miles (5km) west of Scarborough. A steeply wooded, typical glacial meltwater channel through which the River Derwent flows south, the valley is a prime site for bird observation and forms part of a National Nature Reserve. Common species likely to be seen include chaffinch, wood pigeon, tawny owl, jackdaw, lapwing, carrion crow, rook, magpie, blackbird, starling, thrush, greenfinch and many others. Less common are heron, kingfisher, goldcrest, dipper, pied flycatcher, tree creeper, jay, woodpecker, mallard, wood warbler, tree pipit, grey wagtail, turtle dove, nightjar and tits. Even this list is far from comprehensive!

Chaffinch

As one would expect, mammals of the countryside exist in a variety of habitats: foxes, badgers, rabbits and hares, squirrels, hedgehogs, stoats, weasels and moles. Water voles are found widely in stream and river banks, and there are several colonies of bats in the Helmsley district.

(c) The Coast

Boulby Cliff is the highest in England, rising to 700ft (213m) above the sea. The remainder of the Park's coastline also consists of many sizeable cliffs, mostly rocky or of unstable boulder clay subject to serious erosion and offering scant roothold for plants. Coltsfoot, common horsetail and grasses often grow in these locations, with primroses and yellow celandines favouring sheltered, moist places away from the sea. Cliff-tops themselves form the fringe of cultivated land in many sections, but hazel and other tree species manage to survive behind the higher cliffs and in ravines or cuttings.

The call and antics of seabirds form a memorable feature of coastal walking: here are found gulls, fulmars, redshanks, kittiwakes and cormorants, with rock pools and sandy shallows providing a feeding ground for waders. Robin Hood's Bay village is a good viewing area and is readily accessible to visitors. Narrow wooded glens running inland contain numerous woodland birds in common with the dales.

Reefs, rocky ledges and pools support many forms of marine life, although a history of industrial pollution stretching back to the last century has taken its toll and seashore flora and fauna seems less prolific than in some other parts of coastal Britain. Sea fishing between Saltburn in the north and Filey in the south is largely for sea trout, salmon, eels, mackerel and cod. Boat trips run regularly out to the banks and wrecks, while beach angling is best off the sandy beaches south of Bridlington.

Rough seas north of Whitby

APPENDIX 5: Useful Addresses

When writing to any of the organisations mentioned below, please enclose a stamped, addressed envelope.

British Mountaineering Council,
Crawford House,
Precinct Centre,
Booth Street East,
MANCHESTER M13 9RZ

British Tourist Authority,
Information Centre,
64, St. James' Street,
LONDON SW1

British Trust for Conservation
 Volunteers,
36, St. Mary's Street,
WALLINGFORD,
Oxon. OX10 0EU

Camping & Caravanning Club of
 Gt. Britain,
11, Lower Grosvenor Place,
LONDON SW1W 0EX

Countryside Commission,
John Dower House,
Crescent Place,
CHELTENHAM,
Glos. GL50 3RA

Cyclists' Touring Club,
69, Meadrow,
GODALMING,
Surrey GU7 3HS

Department of the Environment,
(Ancient Monuments Commission),
25, Saville Row,
LONDON W1X 2BT

Forestry Commission Headquarters,
231, Corstorphine Road,
EDINBURGH EH12 7AT

for North Yorkshire:

Forestry Commission,
1a, Grosvenor Terrace,
YORK YO3 7BD

Long Distance Walkers'
  Association,
29, Appledown Road,
ALRESFORD,
Hants. SO24 9ND

National Trust,
36, Queen Anne's Gate,
LONDON SW1H 9AS

Nature Conservancy Council,
Northminster House,
PETERBOROUGH PE1 1UA

Nature Conservancy Council,
North-east Regional Office,
Archbold House,
Archbold Terrace,
NEWCASTLE-UPON-TYNE
NE2 1EG

North York Moors National Park,
Information Service,
The Old Vicarage,
Bondgate,
HELMSLEY,
Yorks

North York Moors Railway,
Moors Rail,
Pickering Station,
PICKERING,
North Yorkshire

Ordnance Survey,
Romsey Road,
Maybush,
SOUTHAMPTON SO9 4DH

Ramblers' Association,
1/5, Wandsworth Road,
LONDON SW8 2LJ

Royal Society for the Protection of
  Birds,
The Lodge,
SANDY,
Beds. SG19 2DL

Woodland Trust,
Westgate,
GRANTHAM,
Lincs. NG31 6LL

Yorkshire and Humberside Tourist
  Board,
321, Tadcaster Road,
YORK YO2 2HF

Yorkshire Wildlife Trust,
20, Castlegate,
YORK YO1 1RP

Youth Hostels Association,
Trevelyan House,
ST. ALBANS,
Herts. AL1 2DY

Information Centres

Danby Lodge Moors Centre, tel: (02876) 654
Helmsley Book Shop, tel: (0439) 70775
National Trust Centre, Ravenscar, tel: (0723) 870 138
Ryedale Folk Museum, Hutton-le-Hole, tel: (075 15) 367
Sutton Bank, tel: (0845) 597426
Low Dalby Visitor Centre, tel: (0751) 60295
(Please note that not all Information Centres open outside the summer season - if necessary, check with the National Park Information Service, address above.)

A Country Code for the Moors

Enjoy the countryside and respect its life and work.

Guard against all risk of fire, especially on the moortops in summer. Inform the Police of any fire's location and do not attempt to fight it yourself, unless it is very small.

Fasten all gates.

Keep your dogs under close control, particularly near livestock.

Keep to public paths across farmland, unless re-routed round the edge of crops by a farmer. Where possible, walk in single file.

Respect hedges, walls and fences by only crossing them at gates and stiles.

If you encounter a grouse-shooting party on your route, wait until it is clear to pass or turn back and choose another path. National Park Information Centres should have details of moors being used for shooting.

Leave livestock, farm machinery and growing crops alone.

Pack litter in rucksack or pocket and take it home.

Help to keep all water clean.

Do not disturb wildlife or damage plants and trees.

Take special care on twisting country roads: see and be seen.

Make no unnecessary noise and respect the privacy of local inhabitants.

Cairn on Iron Howe, Bilsdale transmitting mast distant right (Walk 12)

PRINTED BY
CARNMOR PRINT & DESIGN, LONDON ROAD, PRESTON